Immigrants in Children's Literature

Rethinking Childhood

Joe L. Kincheloe and Jan Jipson
General Editors

Vol. 13

PETER LANG
New York • Washington, D.C./Baltimore • Boston • Bern
Frankfurt am Main • Berlin • Brussels • Vienna • Oxford

Ruth McKoy Lowery

Immigrants in Children's Literature

PETER LANG
New York • Washington, D.C./Baltimore • Boston • Bern
Frankfurt am Main • Berlin • Brussels • Vienna • Oxford

Library of Congress Cataloging-in-Publication Data

Lowery, Ruth McKoy.
Immigrants in children's literature / Ruth McKoy Lowery.
p. cm. — (Rethinking childhood; vol. 13)
Includes bibliographical references (p.   ) and index.
1. Children's stories, American—History and criticism. 2. Immigrants
in literature. 3. Emigration and immigration in literature.
4. American fiction—History and criticism. 5. Ethnic groups in literature.
6. Minorities in literature. I. Title. II. Series.
PS374.I48L68   810.9'9282—dc21   99-14231
ISBN 0-8204-4483-9
ISSN 1086-7155

Die Deutsche Bibliothek-CIP-Einheitsaufnahme

Lowery, Ruth McKoy:
Immigrants in children's literature / Ruth McKoy Lowery.
–New York; Washington, D.C./Baltimore; Boston; Bern;
Frankfurt am Main; Berlin; Brussels; Vienna; Oxford: Lang.
(Rethinking childhood; Vol. 13)
ISBN 0-8204-4483-9

Cover design by Nona Reuter

The paper in this book meets the guidelines for permanence and durability
of the Committee on Production Guidelines for Book Longevity
of the Council of Library Resources.

© 2000 Peter Lang Publishing, Inc., New York

Printed in the United States of America

For Saul and Dandre,
the two gems in my life;
and for Henry and Albertha McKoy
who taught me to dream.

Acknowledgment

Immigration in America is an age-old story. Across generations, people have immigrated here from countries far and near. Each immigrant group may tell a different story but there is usually some common thread that links us all—the dream of a better life. In the struggle to ascertain the "American dream," some immigrants' stories get told and others do not. My hope is that we are all cognizant of whose stories are told, how those stories get told, and what those stories tell.

This book represents a major accomplishment that would not have been realized without the help and support of some very special people. I am grateful to my mentors, colleagues, family members, and friends who have aided me in some form or other to take this professional journey.

I wish to thank Patrick Shannon, Joe Kincheloe, Jamie Myers, Aaron D. Gresson III, Shirley Steinberg, Janice Jipson, Rosemary McGarry, Linda Lamme, and Stephen Voss, people who have helped to shape and strengthen my professional journey.

To Bernadette Alfaro, my production coordinator at Peter Lang and the editorial staff, Lisa Dillon, Jacqueline Pavlovic, and Jeff Galas, thank you for helping to make this book a reality.

To my parents Henry and Albertha McKoy, who cheered me on from the beginning, thank you for being there. To Dorothy Vanette, Frances White, Sonia and Lincoln Dillon, Que-My Dillon, Sandra McKoy, James and Icelyn O'Sullivan, and Ionie Williams, thank you. To my brothers and sisters: Lurline, Cecil, Ralvin, Sonia, Mary (Pauline), Paul (Eulem), and Henry who proudly cheered in the backgrounds, thank you. To the True Witness Apostolic church family, thank you for your prayers.

Finally, a special thank you to my husband Saul and my son Dandre. Your love, support, and strong faith have enabled me to accomplish so much. Thank you for being a strong source of strength.

Contents

Foreword

When authors write children's books, they decide, sometimes consciously and often unconsciously, what to include and how to represent their characters and topics. When teachers choose books, they decide, sometimes consciously and sometimes by selecting books with good stories or content to fit the curriculum, how these story characters will be presented to children. Why is this important? In Ruth McKoy Lowery's book *Immigrants in Children's Literature*, immigration is used as an example of how classism and racism impact the writings of authors who write about past events in American history.

For readers who are not well versed in the history of immigration, Ruth leads you through three major historical periods of immigration. She then describes how immigrants from each period are portrayed in novels suitable for upper elementary and middle school children. The majority of the novels are about poor immigrants written to explain how Americans treat "others."

The stories of rich immigrants are rarely heard. It is no wonder that there are those today who view immigrants as a drain on society. In reality, we all are immigrants and it was by immigrant labor and actions that our country became what it is today. Granted Ruth Lowery, herself an immigrant, has a pro-immigrant stance, but her clear descriptions of the content of the books vividly demonstrate her points.

What is wonderful about this book is that it can help teachers read more critically themselves and learn how to interpret stories with an eye to how people of different races, genders, and incomes are presented. That lesson can be applied to all children's books. Further, Ruth Lowery explains why books cannot be left alone to speak for themselves. Children need to be taught to be critical readers as well. They need to question who the author is, and why the author wrote the book the way it was written. How are minority people presented and what are their roles in the story line?

It is not enough to share good immigrant stories with children; we need to be sure that the issue of representation is addressed as children read those fascinating stories. It is not just from the story that readers come away with information and opinions about the groups of people depicted in a book. Curriculum cannot be transformed by merely adding books about immigrant experiences. True reform comes from analyzing how those books depict the immigrant experiences and which experiences authors choose to write about. For any teacher, librarian, or parent who wants a clearer view of what critical theory is all about, this book is a must.

Linda Leonard Lamme

Chapter 1

Immigrants in Children's Literature

We have had far too much immigration in far too few years. We need to ask basic questions: Are we still trying to fill up an empty continent? Does the United States face an acute labor shortage? We have no need for immigration today.
-Dan Stein, executive director of For American Immigration Reform "FAIR" in an interview with *American Legion Magazine* 1995, 26

The first time I read Rosa Guy's novel *The Friends* (1973), it was handed to me by an immigrant fifth-grade student from the West Indies. One morning as I prepared for the approaching school day, Marian[1] knocked on my door. "This is for you, Miss L. You don't have any West Indian stories in the class library so I brought this for you. My sister says it's good." Thanking her and assuring her that I would read the book, I walked away to complete my tasks before the bell. "Miss L.," Marian called, "since you're Jamaican too, I thought you would like it." With that, she smiled and ran off to join her friends. Looking over the novel, I noticed how torn the covers and several of the pages were. I also realized that the book had been borrowed from the library at least two years previously and had not been returned. I immediately thought that the book must be very interesting for my student to bring it to my attention.

Later that day as I began reading the novel, I was intrigued with the plot. *The Friends* tells the story of Phyllisia, a young West Indian girl, who immigrates with her family to Harlem, New York. The story describes her early immigrant experiences growing up in Harlem during the 1960s. Although she is the smartest girl in her class, the students laugh at her accent, calling her a West Indian "monkey." They accuse her of being the teacher's pet because the teacher frequently calls on her in class. The girls she wishes to befriend want nothing to do with an "immigrant," and she herself is embarrassed to be befriended by another outcast in the class, a tough, unkempt girl named Edith who ends up protecting her

---

[1] Name has been changed.

from being the class's punching bag. Phyllisia's father does not hide the fact that he dislikes Edith or anyone who looks like her. He calls her a "ragamuffin" (63) and forbids his daughter to talk to her. However, Edith soon becomes her solace when Phyllisia's mother dies of cancer.

Although, initially, I was happy to read a story based on the West Indian immigrant's experiences, I found the plot somewhat problematic because of the negative imagery portrayed. I was disturbed at Phyllisia's negative experiences and wondered what implications this representation of immigrants could have on my students. After reading the novel, I began to critically analyze the themes that seemed to unfold. The main theme that stood out was that of young immigrant children's quest for cultural identity. These children are caught in a duality between their ethnic culture and the new American culture and do not know how to situate themselves within the two.

As I wondered about the social and political implications of the representations of immigrant children in the novel, several specific questions emerged: Are there other novels that delineate the immigrant experience? What are the common images of immigrants present in children's literature? Are these images always as negative as Phyllisia's experiences in *The Friends* (1973)? How are issues of race and class played out in the novels? How could these representational images impact other students attending school and educators working with immigrant children? Most important, how can representation in these books be deconstructed?

The topic of representations of immigrants in children's literature is of utmost concern and importance to me as a language and literacy educator of young immigrant children from various countries around the globe and of preservice teachers who will ultimately teach these immigrant children. Currently, there are competing representations of immigrants in public discourses. On the one hand, there is the argument that immigrants are no longer needed in the United States because they are a drain on American resources. On the other hand, many still see America as a land of "hope," the Statue of Liberty still representing a welcoming harbor for weary feet. If these differing views are such a paradox for adults to deal with, how does this play out in representations of immigrants for children?

Literature is one medium in which the world is presented to us (Morrison 1992). It thus becomes one of the primary ways in which children are given a view of the world (Banks 1997; Huck, Hepler and

Hickman 1993; Norton 1983). Children see books, or texts, everywhere. They are sanctioned in school and read at home or in the library. Books, then, represent a viable medium for presenting different images and concepts to children.

While we realize the need to present information to children, we must also be cognizant of how this information is presented. After hearing about immigrants from the media, in their homes, or elsewhere, children do develop an image of who or what an immigrant is. School is often the main forum where American children may interact with immigrant children. How they perceive their immigrant peers can directly influence the relationships that may or may not develop. Although the need for presenting information about immigrants through literature is great, there is an even greater need to present positive information that can counter stereotypes.

My critique of *The Friends*, the current flurry of debates on immigrants in America, and my concerns about representations in literature being used with children forced me to look at how immigrants may be represented in other novels. I use the term "representation" to mean an understanding of the "past through the present in order to legitimate and secure a particular view of the future" (Giroux 1994: 47), believing that the written word has a greater influence on humanity than simply reflections of past and present events.

The increasing number of immigrants coming to the United States of America has signaled a need for a greater immigrant-sensitive curriculum (Kellogg 1988; Patrick 1986). This is an important shift in traditional educational attitudes and practices in immigrant education (Roth-stein 1994). However, there is evidence that the traditionally negative values, beliefs, and feelings toward immigrants persist. Hence, consider the epigraph opening this chapter. The realization that these negative sentiments toward immigrants are common among many nativist groups (Nelkin 1995) demonstrates that Phyllisia's experiences as a new immi-grant are not an isolated case in point.

This book employs a critical literacy and sociology of literature theoretical framework to analyze representative materials, namely children's literature, to determine ethnic sensitivity toward immigrant experiences in the United States. In particular, it examines how issues of race and class affect, or influence, representations of immigrants, especially immigrant children, in children's literature and analyzes the implications these representations could have on students and educators as more and

more schools are incorporating children's literature into their language
arts and literature curricula. Critical literacy allows a researcher to view
language as "multiaccentual." Kincheloe (1997) describes this multiaccentual view to mean that language "can be both spoken and heard,
written and read in ways that reflect different meanings and different
relationships to social groups and power formations" (62). I also utilize a
thematic content analysis methodology to investigate commonalities of
these representations in the novels. Issues of race and class are very
important in gleaning an understanding of how different ethnic and racial immigrant groups to the United States are, and have been, portrayed.

Immigration: The Great American Debate

There are two very important issues to consider in the discussion of
immigration. First, the current controversy surrounding recent immigrants and immigration policies, and second, the myth of America or the
"American dream" that still causes people from around the world to
make the hallowed journey here hoping to find their piece of the
"American pie." The current trends in American immigration policies
are very controversial (American Legion 1995). More and more, media
representations portray a negative image of immigrants. Representations
in books are a part of this negative portrayal (Patrick 1986). People may
often wonder about immigrants: Who are they? Where are they from?
How do they affect the American economy? What can be done about
them? These questions are frequently being asked and answered by
researchers on opposing sides of the debate (Ashabranner 1993; Barkan
1996; Beilenson 1996; Heer 1996; Lamm 1995; Sharry 1994; Yans-
McLaughlin 1990). The open arms that once patiently welcomed
immigrants now seem to be closing abruptly. All across the nation, laws
affecting immigrants are being made only to be rescinded in courts.

For example, U.S. District Court Judge Pfaelzer ruled the recent ban
on services to illegal immigrants in California, Proposition 187, uncon-
stitutional on November 14, 1997 ("Judge Rules" 1997). Similarly, the
1996 immigration law that eliminated the privilege for immigrants
awaiting permanent residency approval to remain in the United States
was rolled back by the U.S. Congress on November 13, 1997. In the state
of Florida, Governor Chiles sued the federal government, claiming that
the government is liable for the extra resources Florida has to utilize in

accommodating the various waves of immigrants (DeGeorge 1994). The debate seems endless and thoroughly negative.

America's intolerance of recent immigrants, although the country was built on immigration principles and is regarded as "still a nation of immigrants" (Ashabranner 1993), envelops racial, socioeconomic, and ethnic boundaries. The "browning of America" (Banks 1993), which produced a drastic change in the racial population since the Immigration Reform Act of 1965 eliminated racial and ethnic discriminatory preferences for eligibility for immigrant visas, is very evident in the racial and ethnic makeup of recent immigrants. These immigrants are predominantly Asians, West Indians, and Latin Americans (Rolph 1992) and are often referred to as the "new immigrants" (First 1988; Keely 1986; Kellogg 1988). Ewa Morawska (1990) reports that waves of immigrants are often given the title "new" to distinguish them from earlier immigrants. Historical data shows that the negative treatment of immigrants goes as far back as the earliest American history (Nelkin 1995). As the racial population of immigrants changes, the hysteria heightens concerning who is accepted or denied residency ("All Right, Just This Once" 1994; Nelkin 1995). Descriptions of various immigrant populations are used to represent every member of a particular population. Thus, for example, Mexicans may all be viewed as illegal immigrant aliens coming to the United States to live off the hardworking Californians or Texans. Proposition 187, then, proves to be a necessary measure to keep them out. Thus, representation plays a pivotal role in understanding how immigrants are portrayed and how issues surrounding them are interpreted.

I draw on the discourses of critical literacy and the sociology of literature to evaluate a core set of nineteen novels being used in a local school district's interdisciplinary language arts/social studies unit on immigration. The book does not seek to indict or praise the efforts of the teachers and students engaged in the study of these texts. Instead, the focus is solely on critical interpretations of the contents of the novels and not on issues surrounding why the teachers selected the novels, the process of their selection, whether they make problematic the contents of the books or how the students currently work through their interpretations of the books.

The books discussed are referred to as realistic fiction because they incorporate the history and lived experiences of people from across various historical immigration periods coming to live in the United

States, from the mid-eighteenth century with 1850's Irish immigrants: *Wildflower Girl* (Conlon-McKenna 1991), to 1870's Bohemian immigrants: *My Antonia* (Cather 1918), to 1900's Russian Jewish refugees: *Land of Hope* (Nixon 1992), to 1970's Cambodian refugees: *Children of the River* (Crew 1989), to current Mexican immigrants: *The Crossing* (Paulsen 1987).

As with any major project there is certainly a larger body of reference materials that could be incorporated into the discussion of representations of immigrants in literature. However, while acknowledging that the themes I analyze and elaborate on may be evident in other novels and literary media, my main focus is on the core set of novels. Patrick's (1986) assertion that "stirring stories about the latest immigrants in popular books and magazines contribute strongly to our image as a symbol of hope, freedom and opportunity for a better life," (172) plays a major role in the following discussion. The knowledge unearthed by this study, although it may not be generalizable to all studies, can be pertinent to a wider range of literature explorations.

Theoretical Framework

Young (1996), in her study examining the representations of black people in films, asserts that no one theoretical framework can be employed to address all issues. She further points out that it is sometimes necessary to draw on a number of different theories to achieve this goal. Young classifies this bringing together of different theories as an "interdisciplinary approach." My research uses this interdisciplinary approach, incorporating the critical literacy framework (Anderson and Irvine 1993; Apple 1993; Giroux 1994; Kincheloe and McLaren 1994; Lankshear and McLaren 1993; Shannon 1995) and the sociology of literature framework (Albrecht 1954; Hall 1979; Laurenson and Swingewood 1972).

Critical Literacy

Critical literacy posits that literature is socially constructed. The main goal of this theory is to challenge unequal power relations because it determines that experiences are historically constructed within specific power relations. Critical theory, the roots of which came out of Frankfurt, Germany, which refers to the theoretical tradition developed by the Frankfurt school, still possesses the ability to "disrupt and challenge the status quo" (Kincheloe and McLaren 1994, 138). Kincheloe and McLaren further assert that although the term critical theory is used often, it is frequently misunderstood. A critical researcher must understand the concepts of critical research before a critical analysis can be conducted. Kincheloe and McLaren describe a critical researcher as an individual who:

> attempts to use her or his work as a form of social or cultural criticism and who accepts certain basic assumptions: that all thought is fundamentally mediated by power relations that are social and historically constituted; that facts can never be isolated from the domain of values or removed from some form of ideological inscription; that the relationship between concept and object...is never stable...finally, that mainstream research practices are generally, although most often unwittingly, implicated in the reproduction of systems of class, race, and gender oppression. (139–140)

Giroux (1994) also explicates that the issues that concern a critical pedagogy include the relationships between power and knowledge and between language and experience.

Critical literacy alters the discourse of traditional literacy (Shannon 1995). Shannon points out that critical literacy enables the use of multiple texts to "make sense of one's life and the world in a particular context" (103). This sense-making process enables the exploration of representations of immigrants in literature across various historical periods, looking at how issues of race and class affect these representations. Apple (1993) shares a view similar to Shannon's in that he believes that critical literacy fosters the growth and understanding of all social-life activities we participate in. He determines that there is a relationship between knowledge and the larger society. Anderson and Irvine (1993) further emphasize that the goal of critical literacy is to challenge unequal power relations, as people's experiences are historically constructed within specific power relations. When pooled together these insights on critical literacy provide a solid infrastructure for the type of exploration with which this research is concerned. A critical analysis does not assume that everyone will agree with the findings of any given research, but rather indicates that research findings may be contrary to regularly held beliefs. Critical literacy challenges us to look beyond the regular plot of a story as we seek to find the hidden meanings and/or messages behind the written word.

Sociology of Literature

As the tenets of critical literacy force us to carefully examine various artifacts, so too the sociology of literature theory posits that literature plays an important role in shaping social reality, in that literature reflects society. The principles of sociology of literature command that we critically read literary texts to gain clear insights into the social world. Laurenson and Swingewood (1972) view literature as a "direct reflection of various facets of social structure, family relationships, [and] class conflicts" (13). They argue that the task of the sociologist of literature is to relate the experiences of the imaginary characters and situations to the historical climate they are developed from.

Albrecht (1954) highlights three theoretical assumptions of the relationship of literature and society: Literature reflects society; literature influences society; and literature functions as social control. Literature reflecting society suggests that literature mirrors the everyday occurrences in our lives. Literature influencing society suggests that literature has the power to shape people's lives. The third tenet, literature as social control, suggests that literature maintains an accepted social order that not all participants within a society will find compatible. The most commonly accepted assumption is the "literature as reflection" theory. Albrecht asserts that if literature can reflect, it can also "confirm and strengthen cultural norms, attitudes, and beliefs" (431). Reflection helps the reader to see beyond the written word to look at how the culture, attitudes, and beliefs of the time influence a text.

Hall (1979) challenges us to move beyond the simple concept of reflective literature to the concept that literature is a "social referent" (32). He distinguishes this latter concept by asserting that unlike the former, referent literature suggests that the artist is not a passive agent, waiting to be bombarded with social stimuli, but instead is an active individual concerned with understanding his or her society. The reader brings some sense of awareness to reading the text. Given the highlighted ideology of the critical literacy and sociology of literature theories, both theories can be effectively employed to examine the historical ethnic-sensitive representations of immigrants in children's literature and can show how the usage of these representations may affect students and educators. I refer to the two theories collectively as the "critical sociology of literature."

Children's Literature on Immigration Experiences

The core set of books was also divided into the three immigrant waves to coincide with the time period about which they were written. Of the nineteen books, two were eliminated because they did not speak particularly to the American immigrant experience in the fifty states. They are: *Between Two Worlds* (Lingard 1991), a story of 1940's Latvian immigrants to Canada; and *Going Home* (Mohr 1989), a story of prejudice faced by a young Puerto Rican American girl, born and raised in New York, when her family returned to Puerto Rico to visit their extended family.

Of the seventeen remaining books, four books were classified under the early immigration wave, eight under the middle immigration wave, and five under the new immigration wave. Books in the early immigration wave are: *Wildflower Girl* (Conlon-McKenna 1991), a story of a young Irish girl's voyage to America and her struggles to survive here; *My Antonia* (Cather 1918), about a young Bohemian immigrant and her experiences growing up in the United States; *The Slave Dancer* (Fox 1973), a story of a young boy who is kidnapped and taken to Africa, where he is forced on the return journey to play his fife so the captured slaves will dance; and *Sing Down the Moon* (O'Dell 1970), about the forced migration of the Navaho tribe.

The books in the middle immigration wave are: *Letters from Rifka* (Hesse 1992), a story chronicling the many obstacles young Rifka faces as her family escapes from Russia to travel to the United States; *Journey to America* (Levitin 1987), about a Jewish family's escape from Germany; *Silver Days* (Levitin 1989), the sequel to *Journey to America*; *The Cat Who Escaped from Steerage* (Mayerson 1990), an account of a young Polish girl's journey to America and her struggles to hide her cat from the ship's crew; *Land of Hope* (Nixon 1992), a tale of three young girls from Russia, Sweden, and Ireland and the friendship that blossoms among them as they journey to America; *Good-bye Billy Radish* (Skurzynski 1992), a story of a young American boy and his close friendship with a Ukrainian immigrant boy; *Good-bye to the Trees*

(Shiefman 1993), in which a young Russian girl works hard to send for other members of her family; and *The Star Fisher* (Yep 1991), a tale of Chinese-American immigrants relocating to Virginia and their struggles to gain acceptance there.

Finally, the books in the new immigration wave are: *Journey of the Sparrows* (Buss 1991), a tale of a young Salvadorian refugee and her family's ordeal as they are smuggled across the Mexican border to Chicago; *Children of the River* (Crew 1989), about a young Cambodian refugee, her family's terrifying journey to the United States, and her struggles to be accepted in school; *Kim/Kimi* (Irwin 1987), a story of a young Japanese-American girl's determination to find out about her Japanese ancestry; *The Crossing* (Paulsen 1987), in which an orphaned boy struggles to survive on the streets of Mexico and secretly plans to enter the United States; and *A Boat to Nowhere* (Wartski 1980), a tale of a Vietnamese family's survival at sea as they search for freedom.

The cross-ethnic study of the novels and historical data was intended to delve further into the question of the roles that race and class issues play in immigrant representation in literature. The order of the study was purposefully constructed, as I argue that these two issues have very influential roles in the treatment and representation of immigrants in the United States. The study identifies and makes connections between the ways children of different racial and socioeconomic status are treated within the three documented historical immigrant waves; it also shows how this treatment is reflected in the novels analyzed.

Procedures for Data Analysis

The processes involved in a literary analysis should be thoroughly planned and executed so that conclusions reached can be substantiated. With this belief in mind, several specific analytical techniques were employed to facilitate the completion of this study. The analysis entailed a three-step process. The first step was a brief overview of the three immigration waves: the early immigration wave, 1820–1899; the middle immigration wave, 1900–1964; and the new immigration wave, 1965–present. The three immigration waves show changes in the ethnic and racial identities of immigrants to America and explicate how these different immigrant groups were treated. This step delineates dominant discourses of how immigration was, and is, viewed in the United States in each period. It includes a look at common and uncommon historical recordings of each immigration wave, outlining discriminatory experiences adults and children faced in each historical period.

The second step, which substantiates the major volume of the data analysis, involved the reading and individual analysis of each novel, looking particularly at instances of race and class representations that shed a negative light on immigrants. Each novel was read initially to gain familiarity with the story's plot and characters. Second and subsequent very close readings of each novel were done to answer four main questions. The four questions were broken into more narrow focus areas to account for a wider range of analysis.

1. What are the common representational images of immigrants in children's literature?
   - Who are the immigrants?
   - Where do they come from?
   - What are their experiences before and after they came?
2. How are issues of race and class represented in the novels?
   - How are characters racially identified?
   - Are issues of race and class present in the novels?
   - How are these issues handled?
3. Do these images change for different immigrant groups?
   - How are different immigrant groups presented?
   - How do characters handle cross-cultural encounters?
4. Do these images change for different time periods?
   - Are novels reflective of the historical period they represent?
   - How are images of immigrants represented across the three immigrant periods?

This step further involved a very thorough and timely investigation of all data sources. For example, as I reread each book, I sought to find general themes that were evident in each, using the four questions as my guide in examining the novels. Question four was not used in the individual analyses of the books as it speaks to the broader topic of immigrant experiences across the three periods. This question is dealt with in its entirety in the final chapter. Subsequent specific analytical rereading aligned the common themes found with the four overarching questions guiding the study.

   The third and final step in the analytical process involved a comparative analysis across the set of novels in each section. This step entailed a look at the commonalities between the novels, linking the data with the historical analysis. It delineated evidences of the relationship between the history and the literary representation of people from the particular historic period.

In the chapters that follow, I analyze the issues of race and class in the representation of immigrants in the novels, and how these issues of representation may affect the usage of these books as educators use them to teach children about immigrant experiences. I begin in Chapter 2 with a look at the present discomfort with immigration policies, drawing on present and past historical data of immigrant treatment to delineate the cause for such discomfort. I also review issues of representation, race, and class and their impact on how various ethnic populations in America are portrayed. I complete this chapter by linking the history of immigration with the representation issues discussed. Chapters 3, 4, and 5 consist of an integrated analysis of the three immigrant waves and the novels representing them. The three chapters are arranged chronologically from early immigration to middle immigration to new immigration. The final chapter synthesizes my analysis of the earlier chapters and discusses implications of how the representation of immigrants in the core set of novels may affect their usage in schools' curricula.

Chapter 2

Immigration and the Making
of the United States of America

This chapter provides a chronological history of immigration in the United States and discusses the role of authors in representing that history—to tell stories about immigration as if they were true. Such representations of immigrants, immigration, and those already here are constructions of authors. However, authors do not just speak only for themselves; rather, they mouth different group positions (ideologies) on their subjects. They do so for a purpose, although the politics of that purpose may not be consciously realized.

Immigration is the movement of people from one country to another, while migration is the movement of people within a nation in which they are natives or citizens (Banks 1997). I use the term immigration to incorporate both movements because while many people have migrated within the United States, they immigrated here from some foreign country to which they can still be aligned (for example, Chinese Americans). I also incorporate both voluntary and involuntary movement of people. The history of America has been commonly reported as the history of European immigrants coming to America and carving out a beautiful country that is solely theirs (Banks 1997). As different generations of immigrants arrive on American shores, those of European origins have been able to assimilate, adopting the dominant views and mores of the Anglo-Saxons (Freedman 1980; Ignatiev 1995). This acceptance into the dominant culture did not come readily for some European immigrants now regarded as "whites" (Ignatiev 1995). However, after facing many tough battles, racially, ethnically, and socioeconomically, they were all ingrained in the "white" American culture.

Today's Jewish, Irish, and Italian immigrants, who were originally openly discriminated against, are not readily distinguishable from the northern Europeans who first landed on American shores. Currently, there is a "white" America, consisting of white people from around the world (not just white Anglo-Saxon Protestants) and there is a "minority"

America, which consists of people of all nations who have not been able, or allowed, to lose their ethnicity—for example, African Americans, Asian Americans, and Latin Americans—even with the adoption of the Anglo-Saxon way of life. The roles many of these people of minority status played in the making of America are hard to find in the dominant history books. However, several scholars have made it their mission to let these immigrants' stories, or more accurately their histories, be heard (Banks 1997; Takaki 1993; Zinn 1995).

Ronald Takaki (1993) provides an in-depth look at American history. He asserts that one-third of Americans do not trace their roots back to origins in Europe. His study goes deeply into issues of how Native Americans were treated by whites when they first landed on American shores; how whites took over land owned by Native Americans and these tribes tended to die out swiftly; how Jewish, Italian, and Irish immigrants overcame the prejudicial treatment they faced initially before they were accepted into the white mainstream; how Africans survived the slavery era and still had to fight to be accepted (although acceptance today is still questionable); how Chinese Americans overcame their negative treatment; and how Japanese Americans overcame the stigma of the bombing of Pearl Harbor. His view of American history certainly portrays "a different mirror" (the name of the book) of how real American history has been developed over time.

Another prominent scholar, Howard Zinn (1995) also gives a complete view of American history in the revised edition of *A People's History of the United States 1492–Present*. In his endorsement of Zinn's book, Eric Foner of the *New York Times Book Review* asserts, "Historians may well view it as a step toward a coherent new version of American history" (quote on front cover). Zinn's study delineates a history from Columbus's landing on American shores to his treatment of the Native Americans; from the various uprisings in America that resulted in the "United States" agenda to racial tensions among Americans; to current 1990's policies in American politics. Throughout the discussion of my research study, these important works help to inform and state my position on issues of immigration in the United States.

John Kellogg (1988) suggests that America has experienced three "great migrations" (200): the first great wave, which began in 1820; the second great wave, which began in 1900; and the third great wave, which began in the late 1960s. For the purpose of this study, I refer to these three immigration periods as the early, middle, and new immigration waves. I chose these terms (early, middle, and new) because I wanted terms that coincided with the way the core set of novels used in this study were divided.

The First Great Wave/Early Immigration: 1820–1899

The federal government began keeping immigration records in 1820 (Kellogg 1988). Soon after this date, the first great wave of immigrants reached its peak. Most of the 800,000 immigrants arriving annually in America came from "Great Britain, Ireland, Germany, and Scandinavia" and "were ethnically similar to those [English immigrants] already in residence" (200). In 1803 the British Passenger Act was enacted to discourage further immigration, but in 1825 Great Britain repealed this law. The first group of Norwegians arrived in America after the law was repealed. A series of potato blights in Ireland from 1845 to 1849 forced many Irish citizens to immigrate to the United States. In 1855 Castle Garden, a processing center for European immigrants, was opened in New York to accommodate the great influx of immigrants (Banks 1997).

Many Chinese immigrants also arrived to work on the railroads in California during this period; however, they were discriminated against because they were not white. In 1850 the California legislature passed a "discriminatory Foreign Miner's tax, which forced Chinese immigrants to pay a highly disproportionate share of the state's taxes" (Banks 1997: 443). This tax was intended to limit the number of Chinese immigrants entering the area. By 1880 almost 200,000 Chinese immigrants had arrived in the United States. Kellogg (1988) found that persistent negative reactions from other immigrants, about this increase in Asian immigrants, led to other laws restricting further admissions of Chinese and Japanese immigrants.

The Chinese Exclusion Act of 1882 effectively stopped the immigration of Chinese laborers for over ten years (Banks 1997; Wu 1982). Banks asserts that although "certain classes of European immigrants, such as lunatics, convicts, and idiots, were prevented from entering the United States in the 1800s, the first national group that was totally excluded from the United States was non-White" (92). This of course referred to the 1882 Chinese Exclusion Act banning further immigration from Asian nations.

Other important events helped to shape this period. In 1891, Congress established a Bureau of Immigration to maintain twenty-four inspection stations around the nation (Rolph 1992). Ellis Island, the more readily recognized immigration depot for European immigrants, opened and replaced Castle Garden immigration depot as the main port of entry in 1892 (Banks 1997).

The Second Great Wave/Middle Immigration: 1900–1964

The second great wave of immigration had its greatest increase between 1900 and 1920 (Kellogg 1988). Most of these immigrants came from "central and southern Europe, particularly Italy, Hungary, Poland, and Russia. They spoke no English, they came from rural areas, and most were Catholic" (200). The second wave set numerical immigration records. In addition to large numbers of new immigrants, immigrants from the countries in the first great wave also continued to arrive.

The Congressional Act of 1907 extended the classes of immigrants who were excluded from the United States. Victims of tuberculosis and individuals who had committed certain kinds of crimes were added to the list. Between 1916 and 1919, the movement to "Americanize" aliens, to ensure that they would adhere to the dominant cultural mores, was very widespread. The 1921 Johnson Act signaled a turning point in American history. It established a national quota system that introduced the first numerical limits on European immigration. The 1924 Johnson-Reed Act established further quotas and openly discriminated against southern and eastern Europeans and nonwhite nations (Banks 1997).

Kellogg (1988) articulates that the Great Depression in the 1930s resulted in a lower immigrant population, which was limited even more as World War II progressed. He found that immigration in this period was further slowed by a "collapsed economy and restrictive federal quotas" (200). During the lull, America saw the lowest level of immigrants since the early 1800s. Banks (1987) argues that the reduction in southern and eastern European immigrants was because discrimination against them was intense and very widespread.

The comprehensive Immigration and Naturalization Act of 1952 (McCarran-Walter Act) preserved the national quota system but dropped the Asian (Chinese) Exclusion Act of 1882 (Banks 1997; Rolph 1992). In 1954 the closing of Ellis Island marked the end of mass European immigration. The 1950s saw many other changes in immigration policies. As wars raged around the world, many refugees from the Korean War and from the Hungarian Revolution were given asylum in the United States (Kellogg 1988). Kellogg further notes that during this time many of the immigrants who came to the United States were from Canada, Mexico, and the West Indies.

The plight of millions of European refugees prompted the government to devise means of helping them immigrate to the United States (Easterlin et al. 1982). The Displaced Persons Act of 1948 provided admission of more than 220,000 people over a two-year period. Easterlin et al. further noted that the "refugee acts showed that the exigencies of winning allies in the Cold War, combined with genuine humanitarian impulses, could loosen overall immigration policy" (101). The arrival of the refugees resulted in a greater increase in the nonwhite ethnic population that was now dominating immigration trends in the United States.

The Third Great Wave/New Immigration: 1965–Present

The third great immigration wave began in the late 1960s and continues today (Kellogg 1988). This wave was influenced by the "Immigration and Naturalization Act of 1965, by a series of refugee acts passed between 1961 and 1984, and by foreign and domestic economic and political forces" (201). This wave differs from the first and second waves because a majority of the immigrants were non-Europeans. The new immigrants added to the "minority" population.

The 1965 act, which became effective in 1968, abolished the national origins quota system and loosened the United States's immigration policy significantly. Its enforcement enabled many later acts that have helped to construct how immigration policies are presently being handled. In 1980 Congress enacted the Refugee Act of 1980, which unified and regulated the process of qualifying refugees for admission to the United States. In 1986 Congress offered legal status to two additional groups: long-term undocumented residents and special agricultural workers who had entered the United States illegally. The Immigration Act of 1990 also made significant changes in immigration laws, setting immigration to 675,000 annually.

"Racism" in the Immigrant Debate

Racism is the belief in the superiority of one race over all others. Members of the "superior" race believe they have the right to dominance over all others (Lorde 1984). The issue of racism in America has spawned many debates. Opponents and defenders of the belief that racism is still very present in America today have argued their cases in a variety of media, each side citing stark "facts" to support their claims. Frequently, if an individual believes that racism is still very present in American society, he or she is labeled a liberal (D'Souza 1995). Race is a social construction that has been defined differently across time by people in the same social class and by others whose class position changes (Roediger 1991). According to Gould (1981), racial prejudices may be as old as recorded human history. Thus racism is not an abstract idea or concept as many people often wish to believe. Rather, it is a fact of life that affects many Americans personally (Schiller 1996) and continues to be one of America's main social predicaments (Scheurich 1993). Various nonwhite immigrant groups (usually labeled as "minority" groups) often experience racism in employment, housing, and other cases in which they may come in contact with members of another ethnicity or race—or more precisely members of the dominant culture. These instances are often hidden under an "umbrella" of a different name to prevent acknowledgment.

According to Gresson (1995), the meaning of racism has become "renegotiable." An individual can rationalize a racist behavior, or act, to mean something less traumatic than it would mean traditionally. Thus, as different minority groups experience instances of racism, the aggressors try to find subtle labels that legitimize their actions. Gresson sees humor as one vehicle that provides a means for this renegotiation to take place, asserting that humor neutralizes racial tensions. He further discusses that the "death of official racism" demands a need to define the meaning of various persistent instances of "racist behavior" (180), pointing out that some "Contemporary Americans" seek only to understand what they want to understand about racism.

Gresson (1995) takes the discussion of race a step further construing how the meaning of race changes over time to mean different things and to include different groups of people. In his deconstruction of the word "nigger," he outlines how this word, which was originally employed by white slave masters to degrade enslaved Africans, later:

became a broader metaphor for America's non-dark-skinned victims of oppression in the 1960s and 1970s. From white college students and white females to children and the elderly, the notion of "nigger" became an empathic metaphor for the low status and plight of various non-Black-skinned groups in search of equity and equality. (6)

Gresson's discussion emphasizes that derogatory terms have historically been used to distinguish, and bring together, members of oppressed groups. Thus, today in many black communities, the word is freely used to represent various images of the African American. Some have even justified the frequent usage of the word, arguing that if it is used within the culture it is not offensive. If, however, someone outside of the black culture uses the term it becomes grossly offensive. For the purpose of this discussion, I take Gresson's explanation of the expanding meaning of racial oppression to heart. I use the term race to identify and discuss immigrant people of different ethnic backgrounds, cultural orientations, and country of origin, who at some point in American history were regarded as the "outsiders," the "thems," and the "others." I use these terms interchangeably throughout the remainder of this study.

Today, various racially related incidents have played significant roles in highlighting that racism is not dead (Gresson 1996). The recent trial and acquittal of O. J. Simpson caused a major division between racial groups, especially between blacks and whites. The beating of Rodney King by Los Angeles police officers, and the subsequent riot that followed, illuminated existing tensions between law enforcement and blacks. Susan Smith, the mother who drowned her two sons in a canal and blamed this mishap on a "black man," further intensified racial tensions. The beating and sodomizing of a young Haitian immigrant by members of the New York Police Department intensified the call for justice and equality. More recently, the outrage of many African Americans in New York over the acquittal of four undercover officers who fired over forty times at an unarmed young man fatally wounding him, signifies that the issue of racism that divides many ethnic and racial groups in America cannot be ignored any longer. President Bill Clinton recently chaired a forum that focused on race relations in America, and all across the country other organizations are doing their part to address the issue.

Valli (1995) asserts that the issue of "[r]acism and racial animosity may be worse today than 25 years ago" (120). Zinn (1995) also found that no other country in world history has given the issue of racism the importance it has been given in the United States. Still, issues of race continue to dominate discussions of unity and equality in America. Across time, people have always created racial lines in order to differentiate themselves from others who are, or whom they consider, different. The term race was used to differentiate groups by outward appearances, language spoken, the region of origin, and even head size. The rules are changed for different generations, but the negative principles remain constant.

However, D'Souza (1995) in his book *The End of Racism:Principles from a Multiracial Society* seems to justify the negative cloak of racism. He claims that racial discrimination "as we know it" has declined in American society, and he puts the blame for racial tension on members of "minority" groups. He zealously indulges in a "blame the other" motif, pointing out that

> black cultural pathology has contributed to a new form of discrimination: rational discrimination. High crime rates of young black males, for example, make taxi drivers more reluctant to pick them up, storekeepers more likely to follow them in stores, and employers less willing to hire them. Rational discrimination is based on accurate group generalizations that may nevertheless be unfair to particular members of a group. (24)

This thinking justifies the notion that racial discrimination in American society is acceptable if you can provide a rationale for its presence. Despite D'Souza's justification of racist behaviors and his denial that racism is still dominant in American culture today, various accounts by people from different "minority" groups and the negative sentiments of nativist groups prove that racism is still an American staple.

From the beginning of the United States of America, there have been racial tensions in the "American dream." Racism played a prominent role in deciding who came, where they came from, who owned land, and who became a part of the infrastructure. The first acknowledged immigrants to settle in America were white Europeans. When they came, however, there were vibrant Native American populations already existing across the land (Zinn 1995). The disregard for these people's way of life in America began years before with Christopher Columbus's "discovery" of the Americas in 1492. Various scholars have challenged popular discourses of Columbus's discovery, arguing for the living rights of these early native settlers (Simon 1992). Takaki (1993) argues that the "encounters between Indians and whites not only shaped the course of race relations, but also influenced the very culture and identity of the general society" (10). The way Native Americans were initially treated in their own territory foreshadowed the treatments and experiences of other nonwhite groups. The dominant representations of life in America, however, still portray an existence that began with the first European immigrants.

The issue of race has been transformed over generations of ethnic classifications. At first it was used to differentiate ethnic and religious groups for example, Italians and Jews, but in later years it was expanded to include persons with different skin colors, for example, blacks and Asians (Banks 1997; Ignatiev 1995). Ignatiev further asserts that there is no satisfactory definition of race. People are members of different races simply because society assigns them to those racial groups. Banks also argues that as different ethnic groups replaced each other in an upward mobility movement, the issue of race assumed new meaning. As southern and eastern Europeans attained "acceptable levels" of social mobility and "all whites became one" (266), hostilities focused on nonwhite ethnic groups.

West (1993) declares that most Americans remain trapped in the "dominant liberal views" of race in America. He argues that this narrow view leaves us "intellectually debilitated, morally disempowered, and personally depressed" (4). Mosse (1996) discusses the issue of race from a representational viewpoint. He suggests that racism has "always co-opted familiar ideas of beauty and ugliness, of how men and women should look, and locked them into place" (167).

Again, the issue of race goes back to earliest history. When the Pilgrims first came to New England, in order to justify taking land away from the "Indians," they asserted that the Indians had a "natural right" to the land but not a "legal right" (Zinn 1995). This declaration, then, made everything seem right, irrespective of the fact that the newcomers were hurting those people who were already living here. The effects of racism meant that members of minority status saw some doors slowly opened while others remained firmly closed (McKellar 1994). As blacks gained their freedom and other minority populations (for example, Asians and Latin Americans) were allowed the freedom to enter the United States, racism sometimes took a covert role. The different immigrating groups would experience acts of racism according to the political climate existing at a given time. However, instances of racism still persist, as the opening paragraph of this book suggests.

Dill (1994) points out that racial discrimination restricted the type of work immigrant women were allowed to do. The main job for them was household work. However, while many women used this position as a stepping-stone for other working-class jobs, for black women it was the only type of work they could choose. Thus, while the rights of women were being championed, black women were not initially included in this movement. Blacks were kept subordinated (Gould 1981); thus both racism and classism persisted and continue today. Based on these theories, I use race to mean prejudice directed against groups of people at any point in American history. This prejudice may be based on country of origin, ethnicity, race, or the language spoken. Also, I include skin color variations (skin tones) and physical features.

The Case of "Class" in the Immigrant Debate

Although oftentimes relegated to a nonentity, classism also plays a large role in the American immigration debate. Gresson (1997) declares that class identity and interactions have been downplayed in recent years. Ng (1993) also argues that studies of race and ethnic relations have largely ignored class as one of the "essential constituents of the structuring of these relations" (50). Ng further affirms that class is a process indicating how people construct and alter their relations in terms of the "productive and reproductive forces of society" (50). People use whatever means available to them in this construction. She posits that class goes beyond economic status and is structured around how people relate to each other. Class is made during the course of history. Like race, class deals with how people define themselves in relation to others around them. Thus, it is a social construction. I use the term *class* to refer to the differing levels of economic status (acknowledged and unacknowledged) between different groups of immigrants, taking into account their racial and ethnic identifications, how they are allowed to assimilate into the dominant American culture, where they live, and how they are treated generally by others.

Aronowitz (1992) propounds that class "has always been powerful in the United States....In every decade of the 20th century, visible signs of class combat have been present" (66). He holds that class shapes the fate of the majority of Americans economically, ideologically, and spiritually. Kincheloe and Steinberg (1997) also assert that class is important in understanding social diversity in the United States. They point out that socioeconomic class is defined in relation to the labor process, a process that is always changing as it interacts with social and cultural dynamics.

Characteristics of class are identifiable in the distinction made between the types of Europeans who first landed on American shores. Because the earliest immigrants were essentially of the same race, white Europeans, discrimination against each other centered around issues of class. As the immigration waves changed to include members of minority groups, however, discriminatory practices were dominated by racial attitudes. Discriminatory practices guided who came and who did not, as people had to be healthy and employable (Easterlin et al. 1982).

Although many immigrants came who did not have to suffer the inhuman experiences of being bunked together with hundreds of other similarly situated families, the most common instances of recollection involve voices from the marginalized travelers. Oliver and Newmann (1967) note:

> Down to mid-century the vessels were pitifully small; 300 tons was a good size. Yet into these tiny craft were crammed anywhere from 400 to 1,000 passengers...If they talked of it later, the emigrants almost forgot that there had also been cabins for the other sort of men who could pay out 20 to 40 pounds for passage. Their own world was the steerage. (6)

Classism also differentiated who became masters and servants. Zinn (1995) points out that more than half of the colonists who came to North America in the colonial period came as servants. They were indentured servants, bought and sold like slaves. During the seventeenth century servants were mainly English, while in the eighteenth century they were mainly Germans and Irish. However, Zinn found that after this period more and more slaves replaced the English, Germans, and Irish as the servants of choice.

Although various white ethnic groups gained freedom and were able to work freely, Zinn (1995) asserts that many were kept poor to keep them humble. He notes that class lines between the rich and the poor became sharper as more people immigrated. Takaki (1993) maintains that during the eighteenth century, as Ireland experienced severe famine, farmers had less to give to their children. The dominant practice then was to leave the entire estate to the oldest son. As more children became displaced or disinherited by this practice, more and more Irish citizens immigrated to the United States in search of a better life. Soon they took over the jobs that had been dominated by blacks.

Earlier housing settlements were also first distinguishable by ethnicity rather than by race. In various periods, they would be differentiated as slums, then ghettoes, and more recently, projects. Oliver and Newmann (1967) state:

> Older residents resented and discriminated against later immigrants. New arrivals found themselves pushed into slums which in time became ghettoes. And signs like "No Irish Need Apply" often greeted those who sought to better themselves. (5)

The more immigrants arrived, the lower wages went. This made immigrants already living here upset. The differentiation was made because as different groups immigrated, they would be attracted to areas where familiar ways of living were practiced (Hoerder and Knauf, 1992). Hoerder and Knauf further note that as new immigrants settled where others of their countrymen were already living, they lived much of their lives following their own ethnic traditions and cultural patterns. However, as newer generations were born, this cleaving to ethnic traditions changed. The newer generations identified more with the American culture and sought in every way to distance themselves from the cultures of their parents' homelands. Banks (1997) found that immigrants acquired Anglo-Saxon cultural traits in order to participate fully in the American society. Thus, as ethnic groups gained upward mobility, others replaced them and the cycle continued.

Today, classism still exists on a large scale. Although more people are "assimilated" into the American dream—a college education, a job that places them in the middle class or higher, and a house in a mixed neighborhood—there are still subtle and sometimes not-so-subtle reminders that there are differences in people. For example, in the 1970s as war raged in Vietnam, many Vietnamese refugees were granted asylum in the United States. However, many of the immigrants who were initially allowed to come were highly educated individuals from well-to-do families, who were employed by the U.S. government or other major American industries operating in Vietnam. Their passage into America was smoother than many immigrant categories. Many entered with minimal immigration security checks and were sponsored by organizations that helped them acclimate to the U.S. culture; many found jobs with the parent company they worked for in Vietnam. However, as the war continued, the class of Vietnamese refugees changed. These refugees were no longer American employees, they knew little or no English, and they looked like they would become wards of the state. The welcoming atmosphere changed. Although many were allowed to immigrate, they now had to prove that they would be suitable citizens for the United States before they could be sponsored by an organization such as a church (Kelly 1977). The sponsoring organization was still responsible for making them fit citizens, capable of surviving on their own in the United States.

Examples of this nature illuminate for us how perceived differences in people can create major "Berlin Walls" between those who have and those who do not, or those who are accepted and those who are not. Discriminatory acts of classism, acknowledged or not, categorize people in various groups and seek to keep them in these ascribed groups. Thus, Ng (1993) urges us to expand our understandings of class issues beyond the "economic realm" (57). She posits that class in this way of thinking is an "embodiment of ideological and economic processes that structure how people relate to each other socially as well as how they are able to think about social relationships" (57). Roediger (1991) also determines that the task of historical study of race and class is not to draw distinct lines separating race and class, but instead to connect the relationship between them. Again, I use the term *class* to refer to socioeconomic status of different groups of immigrants, taking into account their racial and ethnic identifications, how they are allowed to assimilate into the dominant American culture (changing from immigrant to American), where they live, and how they are treated generally by others.

Representation and Immigrant Literature

An author's job is to represent the world to people. Authors make choices about representational images based on their ideological positions. They then present their findings as truths. Representation is defined as "the act of representing or state of being represented; something, as a picture, that stands for or depicts something else" (Braham 1996: 564). When an idea or concept is used to signify something, we get the sense that this idea or concept can generally be used as a referent for all future representations. For example, when we hear of Proposition 187, our minds may conjure up images of illegal

Mexican immigrants draining government resources in California and the government insisting that it would not allow this to happen any longer. Proposition 187 would give that state the right to deny aid to all illegal immigrants, including their American-born children. Thus, when the word "Mexican" is used, we may think of Proposition 187 and of illegal immigrants and even of California.

Kincheloe (1997) posits that representation deals with the way people, places, and things are depicted within forces of ideology. There is no truly objective way of seeing or interpreting. What seems real is a construction of our minds, and our knowledge of the world has to be interpreted. He argues further that representations are never innocent. They are always inscribed by power and this power has the ability to shape our representation of the world in particular patterns. Immigrants, however, generally do not get to create their own representations. Others create a representational image for them. People can become so affected by these created representations that they adopt them as the norm. Thus we hear the outcries from supporters of Proposition 187 and people like D'Souza (1995) arguing that such outcries are legitimate and are not evidence of bigotry.

Giroux (1994) asserts that representations are built through an understanding of the past to the present. This understanding legitimizes and makes concrete a particular view of the future. In order to understand the future, we must first understand the past and the present. Representation must be understood in its historical and cultural context. This understanding then can shape how we perceive the future.

Because immigrants are often misrepresented in the media (Young 1996), an understanding of how representation affects our interpretation of the world around us is important in understanding how, and why, we view immigrants in these various media. Critical analyses have often been concerned with representations and the relationship between "external reality" and "the image constructed of this reality" (8). Humans have always desired "authentic" representations that highlight real-life experiences (Young 1996). Books are one such form of realism providing a window on these real-life experiences. Banks (1997) argues that books representing the immigrant experience can help make the concept of immigration meaningful and real. For many students, books provide alternative representational images of immigrants that they might not otherwise be exposed to.

An understanding of how representation is portrayed in literature discussions helps as a researcher deconstructs the meanings he or she interprets from reading representative materials on any given topic. On the discussion of images of immigrants in literature, this understanding of representation is no less important. Young (1996) asserts that it is important to trace the development of images, placing them in their historical context. The method of integrating a discussion of the history of immigration with the thematic analysis of the novels dealing with immigrant populations acknowledges this development. The ways images are presented adversely affect their representation.

People often identify with representations that they are either comfortable with or that help to deepen their understanding of themselves or people like them (Gresson 1997; Macedo 1994). Critical literacy forces us to move beyond an acceptance of these comfortable representations to embrace representations that are problematic for us. It challenges us to interpret our knowledge of the world around us. Hade (1997) points out that interpretation is our tool to understanding text. He argues that reading is social and is dominated by culture. The meanings we have about race, class, and gender, even though they may be stereotypes, determine how we interpret text. Kincheloe (1997) argues that cultural identity is formed and informed by a nation's literature.

The ongoing demand for literature that addresses minority groups in the United States has seen the increase in usage of books representing various racial and ethnic peoples (Harris 1991; Nelson and Myers 1993; Shannon 1988; Sims 1982). However, various researchers have argued that the number of books available to children and the quality of representation in the books are questionable (Huck et al. 1993; Reimer 1992; Shannon 1988). In their study on books about minority populations, Huck et al. note that the representations are scarce and many are stereotypical. They determine that the need for more contemporary, realistic fiction is urgent, as the few good books (for example, on Asians—with the exception of many Laurence Yep novels) are mainly based on past experiences. Because educators and prospective teachers may not be getting the ethnic-sensitive materials needed to make the necessary curriculum reforms, various researchers (Banks 1987, 1994a, 1994b, 1995, 1997; Bennett 1995) have developed or further advanced techniques for addressing these issues. A critical analysis of the issues of representation, then, should inform us about the images of immigrants being presented in children's literature and should also offer some ideas on pedagogical implications for using this type of literature with children. Another goal of this analysis should be to ascertain why the representations of immigrants' history are the way they are. The analysis needs to address the issues of race and class, as both issues affect the way history, and the retelling of that history, are formed and interpreted. Issues of race, class, and gender become more obvious when books are compared. The representation in one book that may initially seem simple when it is read in isolation could become problematized when compared to another book that represents a different perspective (Hade 1997).

Importance of Race, Class, and Representation in the Immigration Debate

Books have the power to promote favorable attitudes, to foster positive behaviors in readers, to make us more human, to help us learn to empathize with others, and to show us the past in ways that illuminate the present and the future (Short and Pierce 1990; Sims 1983). However, May (1995) posits that simplistic books have several unfortunate consequences in that they may cause one generation to view certain attitudes or ideas from a particular point of view. She further points out that children who learn from these books become adults who hold certain prejudices as truths. Thus, Banks (1997) urges us to chose books of high quality that do not seek to replicate stereotypes but ones that move beyond the common mainstream views to uncommon realms. As previously noted, the main focus of this work is to critically analyze representations of immigrants, especially race and class issues, in a core set of children's books.

One reason for this focus has been the current demand for more incorporation of literature reflecting diverse cultural experiences in schools' curricula. A more pressing reason for this focus is the need to understand how these images of immigrants are portrayed in these books, seeking an understanding of whether these images are positive and/or negative representations. I use the terms *positive* and *negative* to mean attributes that present either a good or bad image. Like many adults, American children may think of people of minority status when the term "immigrant literature" is mentioned. When they hear of immigrants, the common images that are presented in current media may be their only reference. If adults are struggling with the idea of immigrants in America, it is only fair to question how children may deal with the subject.

For many children, their only contact with immigrants (since many of their families may be white and have assimilated within the dominant American white culture, these children may not view themselves as immigrants) may be through representations in children's literature. We already know that images of immigrants in popular media are frequently negative; images of immigrants in children's literature, however, are not so readily available.

Literature reflects the social concerns of the time and place in which it is created (Nodelman 1992; Sims 1982). Peim (1993) determines that we cannot understand literature without references to social forms. Consequently, in order to conduct an investigation of different representations of immigrants over any time period, it is necessary to understand the history of that time period (Norton 1983). However, sometimes events in history that are delineated in a particular book may not be readily available in dominant historical recordings. Common history may reflect only the views of the dominant cultures within a society (Banks 1997). Since many of the literary texts written about immigrant experiences do not reference the experiences of dominant cultures, but rather those of cultures that would otherwise be underrepresented, it was necessary to unearth alternative views of history, views that have been far too long ignored. Grunfeld (1997) asserts that history is a disputed terrain, that there is not one singular history but rather multiple histories. History has authors who represent what they take to be true. History, then, is literature.

In order to understand the disputed terrain of history, we must have an understanding of how representations influence our connections of social and literary ideas. Since representations help us to understand the past, which in turn helps us to understand the future, they provide a viable understanding of how history informs our daily lives. It is through representational images that we are able to glimpse a view of what was and is. Issues of race and class also play prominent roles in how a culture's history is recorded and later retold. Therefore, in order to understand how images of immigrants are represented in literature, it is necessary to understand the history of the time period the literature addresses, to know what representation is and how it affects our memory recollections, and to understand issues of race and class and their indictment of available historical recordings.

Chapter 3

The Early Immigration Wave: 1820–1899

The "first great wave" or early immigration period reached its peak soon after the federal government began to keep records in 1820 (Kellogg 1988). The majority of the 800,000 immigrants arriving annually came from Great Britain, Ireland, Germany, and Scandinavia. These immigrants were ethnically similar to earlier immigrants who were already settled in the United States in that they spoke English and shared a common culture. This population dominated and shaped the course of immigration through to the early 1900s.

The 1830s saw an increase in the number of new immigrants arriving on American shores. In the 1870s most immigrants were from Germany and Scandinavia while by the 1890s most were from southern and eastern Europe. This period also saw a dramatic change in the number of Chinese immigrants, who were lured from their homelands with tales of "Golden Mountains" in California (Brownstone 1988a). Africans were still being enslaved even though the slave trade legally ended in 1808. Sixty percent of immigrants for most of the nineteenth century were working-age men (Easterlin et al. 1982). Many left their homelands in search of better livelihoods for themselves and their families, hoping to return home after they amassed some wealth.

Federal immigration policy-making began in 1875 (Rolph 1992). Before this date, Congress and the states shared equal responsibility. During the second half of the nineteenth century, however, thirty-three states established their own immigration offices to attract newcomers as their expanding frontiers demanded more manpower (Easterlin et al. 1982). For example, in 1874, Mennonite (Amish) immigrants were entreated to come to the United States with the promise that they would not have to serve in the military. In 1875, Congress enacted the first federal statute to prevent the entry of criminals and prostitutes (Rolph 1992). This was only the beginning, as Congress established other exclusionary clauses in later years to further regulate the categories of immigrants it did not want in the country: convicts and people likely to become public charges. By 1891 Congress had established the Bureau of Immigration, taking control of immigration enforcement away from the states.

Banks (1997) describes several important events that helped to shape this immigration period. As the racial makeup of immigrants changed from purely northern and western Europeans to include eastern and southern Europeans, Asians, and more African slaves, nativists' discontent with outsiders coming in and taking their jobs ran high. They wanted to reclaim America for white immigrants only and did not appreciate other people joining them to hunt for their fortunes. In 1830, the Removal Act was enacted to force Native Americans from their homelands. Between 1846 and 1848, the potato blight in Ireland caused thousands of Irish citizens to immigrate to the United States. In 1850, Chinese immigrants were forced to pay a Foreign Miners tax. This tax unfairly pressured them to pay a large proportion of California's state taxes and was enacted to limit further mass Chinese immigration into California. By 1863, President Lincoln issued the Emancipation Proclamation, freeing slaves in states that had previously refused to free them; in 1869, the transcontinental railroad was completed, improving interstate communication.

Who Are They?: People in the Early Immigration Wave

Although immigrants from many European countries were still arriving in the United States during the early immigration wave, this chapter focuses on the groups that are discussed in the novels being analyzed. Many immigrants in the early 1800s came for economic reasons (Ziegler 1953). Many Europeans in these immigration waves came initially because they heard of the vast amount of farmland they could buy at very low rates, while many Irish immigrants came because famine was ravaging their country and leaving was their most feasible choice. Chinese immigrants came in search of fortune, while Africans came as slaves. The French were some of the founders of the new country; thus, their status is more mainstream than the other immigrant populations mentioned above.

This chapter focuses on the Africans, Chinese, French, Irish, and Native Americans, looking more closely at the Chinese and the Irish, who immigrated in greater numbers from 1820 to 1899. Overall, the immigrants who came to the United States, except the Africans, came because they had dreams of a better life for themselves and their families.

The French in the Early Immigration Wave

The French were some of the earliest settlers to call the Americas home. Kunz (1966) posits that while other nations sent out explorers who only "touched the fringes of the North American continent," the French were "the first Europeans to plunge inland, to stand upon the soil of America's 'heartland'" (8). The French are credited with founding Chicago and Detroit, two of America's greatest cities. Their influence is still widely evident across the United States, from the names of streets, rivers, small towns, and big cities, to a variety of foods, wines, and everyday customs. Theirs is overwhelmingly not a "minority" status.

Many French settlers did not stay in America but rather returned home to France. Kunz (1966) notes that before the English settlers came, the French settled in and quickly learned the Native American way of life: "They lived with the Indians, married Indian women, learned from the Indians the ways of the beaver and muskrat…the French also treated the Indians better than did most white men from other nations" (21). Their stronghold on North America ended when the English settlers arrived.

When the war between the French and British settlers ended in 1759, Great Britain gained most of the land, while most of the French settlers who were left moved to Quebec, Canada, a province that today still has a strong French influence. Those who remained mingled with the new settlers as they had done with the Indians and soon most traces of their French identity, although not their strong legacy, were lost.

The African "Slave" in the Early Immigration Wave

The history of the African in the United States also dates back to the earliest settlement patterns of the Europeans, but it is a history that is mostly filled with bitter recollections. Banks (1997) ascertains that the Africans' experience in America is a unique one. Although among the earliest settlers, they were gradually enslaved in North American colonies as more and more European plantation owners sought free and cheap labor. During the 1800s slavery continued to flourish; thus, when the slave trade was legally abolished in 1808, illegal slave trading began. Jackson and Landau (1973) assert that by 1800 there were over one million slaves working on Southern plantations. While white owners desperately needed the slave labor, they often worried that the slaves outnumbered them. The threat of a slave rebellion always seemed imminent.

Zinn (1995) delineates the life of the African slave in America. He finds that family "solidarity" was very strong among slaves and carried over into the twentieth century. The "slaves hung on determinedly to their selves, to their love of family, their wholeness" (174). In their resentment of the unfair treatment by their masters, many slaves would pretend to be sick, destroy tools, and do anything that would slow the production of goods. They were very careful, however, because they knew that without warning their masters could sell them to other slave masters in faraway states and they would never see their families again.

During the 1800s, freed slaves, and others concerned with the plight of those still in slavery, fought for the abolition of slavery. However, the battle for freedom seemed endless when in 1861 Lincoln, in his first inaugural speech, asserted: "I have no purpose, directly or indirectly, to interfere with the institution of slavery in the States where it exists" (Zinn 1995: 184). Eventually, the 1863 Emancipation Proclamation declared slaves free.

Although negative sentiments toward Africans continued throughout this immigrant period, other legislative laws were made to improve their lives. In 1866 the Fourteenth Amendment gave African Americans the right to be American citizens; the 1866 Civil Rights Act gave them "civil liberties" in several areas; and the 1870 enactment of the Fifteenth Amendment gave them the right to vote.

Native Americans in the Early Immigration Wave

Like the African American, the Native American's life in the United States has been fraught by "racism, discrimination, protest, and resistance" (Banks 1997: 136). Banks further outlines that when Christopher Columbus and his voyagers arrived in America and found the different groups of people already living across the North American continent, they collectively called these people "Indians." The wars that were later waged by and against these people for their lands wiped out many tribes and continued to eliminate other groups well into the 1800s. Of this war over land, Zinn (1995) reports that the "Indian Removal, as it has been politely called" (124), cleared the land for cotton crops, immigration, canals, railroads, new cities, and the building of a massive empire across the continent of the Pacific Ocean.

In 1820 there were 120,000 Native Americans living east of the Mississippi, but by 1844, fewer than 30,000 remained (Zinn 1995). As white settlers craved more land, the tribes lost their beloved lands and were marched off to reservations that these white settlers deemed suitable for them. Many did not go without putting up a fight, but ultimately, the white settlers with their more advanced weapons proved to be too much for these Native people.

The Chinese in the Early Immigration Wave

Chinese immigrants came to America for various reasons. Takaki (1993) found that many sought sanctuary from intense conflicts in their homeland, others fled the turmoil of peasant rebellions and harsh economic conditions, and still others, who learned about "Golden Mountain" left their villages behind with dreams of a better life. A large number of Chinese immigrants were also brought to California as contract laborers to build American railroads (Banks 1997; Easterlin et al. 1982; Kellogg 1988).

At first the Chinese were welcomed in California, but this welcome quickly changed as people feared they would lose their jobs to nonwhite immigrants. The nativists' cries of "California for Americans" led to the 1850 legislative enactment of the Foreign Miner's Tax (Takaki 1993). This tax was aimed solely at Chinese immigrants, requiring individuals to pay three dollars. The law was later repealed but was reinstated in 1852. It remained in force until it was voided by the 1870 Civil Rights Act. Many Chinese immigrants became miners, but when mining profits decreased they soon joined other Chinese working on the railroad.

Negative attitudes toward Chinese immigrants proved that they were discriminated against mainly because of the color of their skin. Although the Chinese arrived at the same time as the Irish immigrants (Takaki 1993), they did not enjoy any privilege invoked by the 1790 citizenship law as the Irish immigrants did. Although today Chinese immigrants, or

Chinese Americans are regarded as "the model minority" (Bandon 1994), their industrious nature was not respected during the early immigration wave. Takaki (1993) determines that overall the role of Chinese immigrants in the history of America has been largely downplayed or disregarded.

The Irish in the Early Immigration Wave

The names "Irish" and "Scotch-Irish" are used to distinguish Irish-American Catholics from Irish-American Protestants, respectively (Brownstone 1989). Brownstone found that the Scotch-Irish name was used in the 1750s but was fully adopted in the 1840s by Irish-American Protestants who wished to distance themselves from Irish Catholics arriving during the famine and plague years of the late 1840s. Irish Catholics, who were usually poor, were more likely to be discriminated against, especially because of their religious faith. My focus in this book is on the "Irish" immigrants who arrived in the 1840s.

In *How the Irish Became White*, Noel Ignatiev (1995) describes how early Irish immigrants were treated when they arrived in America and the role they played in later influencing American history. Early living conditions in Ireland were comparable to those of an American slave. When the Irish immigrants arrived in the United States, the majority of them had to find low-level jobs in order to survive. In the North many men became hard laborers, while in the south they were frequently given dangerous jobs in places where slave owners did not want to risk the lives of their slaves. The women found work mainly as household domestic workers. Their living conditions were deplorable and they were frequently thrown together with free Negroes; they lived in the same areas and essentially fraternized together. Thus, many experienced and understood the plight of the African "immigrants."

Earlier generations of immigrants who had already assimilated into the dominant American culture did not want the Irish immigrants to be included in the American "melting pot" (Ziegler 1953). The Irish became the target of American nativists' hostility because they were a largely Catholic group trying to settle in a predominantly Protestant society (Takaki 1993). They were also the first immigrant group whose living condition was labeled "urban ghetto." The Italians, Poles, and other southern and eastern European immigrants later shared these experiences.

The Naturalization Law of 1790, which was enacted to reserve citizenship rights to white immigrants, later proved adaptable for Irish immigrants because of their similarity in skin color to the members of the dominant culture (Ignatiev 1995; Takaki 1993). Ignatiev asserts that the Irish, who were an "oppressed" race in Ireland, soon became a part of the "oppressing" race in America. When the Irish became accepted as white, they "ceased to be green" (3). Irish immigrants could now live where they wanted, do what they wanted, vote, and be judged by a jury of their peers (Brownstone 1989).

The way the Irish were initially treated in America implies that this "at first we don't like you but soon we will allow you to be like us" mentality was extended to all immigrant groups who arrived in America. This assumption of a change in attitude was true for some immigrant groups but proved erroneous for others, especially if their ethnicity and racial backgrounds—or more pointedly their skin color—was different from that of white immigrants. Two groups for which this assumption proved false were African-American and Chinese immigrants. They were, and still are, considered to be "outsiders," the "thems," or the "others". As different groups, especially those from eastern and southern Europe and nonwhite immigrants, kept coming ashore they experienced the same, and often worse, treatment that these early immigration groups experienced. They have to go through the "rites of passage" before they are allowed to partake in the American dream.

Novels in the Early Immigration Wave: 1820–1899

Four novels address immigration experiences in the early immigration period. *My Antonia* (Cather 1918), *Wildflower Girl* (Conlon-McKenna 1991), *The Slave Dancer* (Fox 1973), and *Sing Down the Moon* (O'Dell 1970) relate tales of immigrants from Bohemia, Ireland, Africa, and Arizona respectively. Each tale weaves a fabric of love lost and regained. Each in its own way provides an important insight into the early immigrant experiences and provides valuable lessons about the histories of the different ethnic groups that immigrated in this period.

Synopses of the Early Immigrant Novels

Cather, Willa. (1918). *My Antonia*. New York: Houghton Mifflin. 244 pp.

My Antonia is a story told through the eyes of Jim Burden, who reminisces about his childhood growing up in Nebraska with his grandparents. At age 14, Antonia Shimerda immigrates with her Bohemian family to Nebraska. Longing for his homeland, Antonia's father commits suicide soon after arriving. Antonia struggles along with her family to survive the harsh realities of poverty in America.

Conlon-McKenna, Marita. (1991). *Wildflower Girl*. New York: Puffin. 173 pp.

Thirteen-year-old Peggy O'Driscoll, orphaned and made homeless by the Great Famine of the 1840s, journeys to Boston from Ireland with hopes of finding a better life for herself. She struggles to maintain her dignity amid various negative experiences and determines to be successful in her new homeland.

Fox, Paula. (1973). *The Slave Dancer*. New York: Bantam Doubleday Dell. 152 pp.

Young Jesse Bollier often played his fife at the New Orleans docks to earn a few pennies. One night he is kidnapped and carried aboard a slave ship on its way to Africa. Jesse is expected to play his fife so the slaves can "dance" to keep their muscles strong and improve their marketability. Jesse soon realizes what he has to do in order to survive and hopefully return home safely to his mother.

O'Dell, Scott. (1970). *Sing Down the Moon*. New York: Bantam Doubleday Dell. 124 pp.

Bright Morning, a young Navaho girl, recounts her experiences of being captured by Spanish slavers and sold into slavery. She escapes with the help of a new friend and returns home. Soon after her return, however, her tribe is forced to live in an enclosed area where they are guarded by white settlers.

Individual Analysis of the Early Immigrant Novels

My Antonia by Willa Cather (1918)

***Race Representations in* My Antonia.** I identified five instances of racial representations that exemplify the assumption that racial issues played major roles in how early immigrants were regarded. When Antonia and her family first arrived in Nebraska, they could not communicate with the natives living there because they could not speak English. The issue of "difference," of "you're not like us," comes across forcefully.

The Shimerdas were unprepared for the changes they experienced. They came to a new country but they did not know how to communicate in that country's dominant language. Their strong distrust of those who were not like them left them open to be deceived by their own countrymen. The people they trusted, who were also immigrants, were the ones most likely to rob them. The Burdens' farm hand, Otto, could have warned them that they were being swindled but the Bohemians had a "natural distrust" of Austrians. The allusion here is that members of your own race are the ones to be distrusted.

After arriving in Nebraska, Mr. Shimerda met two Russian immigrants who, like him, were happy to finally meet someone they could befriend. They shared a common language and were equally outsiders. The Russians were called Pavel and Peter because their last names were "unpronounceable." Their exotic descriptions communicate that they were very different from the American settlers in Nebraska: "Pavel, the tall one, was said to be an anarchist….Peter, his companion, was a very different sort of fellow; short, bow-legged, and as fat as butter" (24).

The men's physical descriptions portray them as exotic creatures, totally different from the "normal" people around them. Pavel has a bad attitude, gets angry at people, and is violent. Peter, on the other hand, is plump and buttery; he is depicted as clownish. Regardless of his pleasant disposition, no one tried to befriend Peter before Mr. Shimerda came. The idea that people who are similar should stick together comes across very strongly.

African Americans are also depicted negatively. We are introduced to a famous blind singer named Blind d'Arnault. He is portrayed as a "heavy, bulky mulatto, on short legs" (118). D'Arnault is described in terms of his race and not his talent. He has a "soft, amiable Negro voice...with the note of docile subservience in it. He had the Negro head, too; almost no head at all....He would be repulsive if his face had not been so kindly and happy" (118). D'Arnault seems to be the model by which all "Negroes" are judged.

He is described as barely having a head, with only skinfolds behind his ears. His voice conveys an image of Negroes as docile and subservient. However, he has one good trait. His otherwise "repulsive" character is made acceptable because his face is "kindly" and "happy." This description of the African American implies that if an individual of African descent does not have a kindly and happy disposition, he or she is repulsive.

This image of African Americans certainly contributes to the stereotypes that were held and are still being held: They are inferior creatures with childish dispositions and are predictable human beings. D'Arnault's stereotypical character is further described. He performed and enjoyed himself as "only a Negro can" (121). Negroes are seen as simple people who love to have fun. The things that cause them pleasure seem unique to them. Thus they enjoy themselves as only "Negroes can."

The American settlers were those of European Protestant descent who had settled in Nebraska in the earliest immigration periods. Their children, especially their daughters, were treated differently from the immigrant children who settled in the area later, and those differences were openly acknowledged. Although the American farmers had the same financial problems as the new immigrants, they are portrayed as caring for their children enough that they refuse to have them do menial labor. In order to maintain their beauty the girls stayed indoors.

The immigrant girls, however, did not have this luxurious choice. Many were hired out to other people's houses, inns, or farms. Their wages for the most part were sent back home to help the family pay off the debt on their property, buy machinery for the farm, and to help the family in general. Although this practice helped the immigrant farmers to be the first to become prosperous, it did not improve their status with the other farmers.

***Class Representations in* My Antonia.** The issues of class representations in *My Antonia* are very distinct. Like the instances of racial discrimination, class issues run deep along the racial division and socioeconomic status of the Americans and the immigrants. Poverty stands out forcefully. Although the Shimerdas arrived together as a family from their homeland, were able to purchase a farm and animals, and had a little bit left over for planting crops the next year, they still fell immediately into poverty. When the cold winds of winter came, they were unprepared. They had one overcoat among them and they took turns wearing it. This leaves the reader to wonder about the industriousness of Mrs. Shimerda. How could a mother not know how to protect her family from the cold? One is further tempted to question her abilities as a housewife. Why did her family not have eggs and chicken like the American families? Grandma Burden ponders, "I've come strange to a new country myself, but I never forgot hens are a good thing to have, no matter what you don't have" (48). The class difference is obvious. Some people immigrate and are able to fall back on resources learned in their homelands while others seem to always be in need of someone showing them how to survive.

Grandma Burden took particular interest in Antonia, teaching her how to cook and helping her to acclimate to American life. When Mr. Burden retired and the family moved to town, she found work for Antonia as a cook with their neighbor, the Harlings. Mrs. Burden was concerned that Mrs. Shimerda would allow Antonia to grow up to be a rough country girl. She felt that Antonia was destined for a better life and did everything she could to ensure it. She is the white savior who wants the best for her humble charge. Without her interference, Antonia would grow up to be a country girl who had no knowledge of the "finer things in life." Mrs. Shimerda, on the other hand, comes across as an irresponsible mother who does not make the welfare of her daughter a top priority.

The obvious difference in class also comes across in the comparison of Jim Burden and a young Norwegian boy. While the young immigrant child is busy finding a job to help his family, Jim is able to laze around enjoying his childhood years. Again, the different images of how immigrant families and American families prioritize their family affairs show a disparity between them.

Jim's revered status is further epitomized when he became the valedictorian of his graduating class. His friends, the immigrant country girls, came specifically to hear him deliver his speech. Afterwards, one of the girls remarked longingly: "It must make you very happy, Jim, to have fine thoughts like that in your mind all the time" (147). Only the people who went to school had the ability to speak well. For these immigrant girls who had to work to help their families, schooling was merely a dream. However, they genuinely found pleasure when one of their own, another immigrant, became a schoolteacher, "Just think! She'll be the first Scandinavian girl to get a position in the high school. We ought to be proud of her" (154). Selma (the schoolteacher) is the first to move away from the stereotypical image of an immigrant girl as a seamstress, housemaid, or mother of many children.

Summary of Race and Class Representations in My Antonia. Racism in this novel is brought out in the way members of different immigrant groups are portrayed. The immigrants are portrayed as distrusting and sometimes ungrateful. Regardless of the way they acted, the Americans (like Grandfather Burden) tried to be patient with them and continued to help them acclimate.

Class issues show distinct differences between the immigrants and the Americans. While the immigrants' children had to go out to work to help support their families, the American children stayed at home, went out with friends, and were able to enjoy their childhood.

Wildflower Girl by Marita Conlon-McKenna (1991)

Race Representations in Wildflower Girl. Although the characters in this novel are all white, issues of race are evident. Looking back at the early categorization of racial groups when the Irish were not considered white, this difference in race becomes more evident. Peggy's first encounter with differences occurred when she found her second job and met Mrs. Rowan, the mistress of the house, for the first time. Peggy marveled at her hair, her small and even teeth and her genteel appearance (99).

Mrs. Rowan's "beauty" seems to stand out for Peggy. Her face is "gentle" and her teeth are immaculate. Immediately, one wonders about the women Peggy grew up with. Didn't any of these women have even, white teeth, or wavy hair? For Peggy, "Elizabeth Rowan was the prettiest woman she had ever seen in her life. Her skin was clear, without a blemish or freckle. Peggy wrinkled her nose thinking of the bridge of freckles that no amount of scrubbing would remove" (106–107).

Peggy traveled to America on a ship with hundreds of women native to her country, yet she had never seen any woman as beautiful as Mrs. Rowan. She immediately compares her own "freckled" features to those of Mrs. Rowan. Obviously she, Peggy, was not beautiful; after all, she couldn't scrub the freckles away.

Peggy seems to be superficially concerned with other people's beauty, something she doesn't see in her culture. These images of beauty convey the message that "beauty" is awarded only to some people. Obviously, from Peggy's longing stares, this beauty was not bestowed on her or other Irish women.

Class Representations in **Wildflower Girl.** The issues of class were more readily identifiable in the analysis of the novel. Not only was Peggy besieged by differences in racial backgrounds, her status as an immigrant from a lower socioeconomic background was also a constant reminder of who she was and how she should behave around people of "means." When Peggy began her job at the Rowans' estate, she was warned that she was different from the Rowans. She must keep her dreams and spirit to herself because a "good capable girl is what they want and that's what they'll get" (98).

The cook, a fellow Irish, also reminded Peggy that their world and that of the Rowans were "worlds" apart. Mrs. Rowan and women like her were not born to live their lives in the kitchen, but Peggy and Mrs. O'Connor (the cook) were ideal for this job. Although Mrs. O'Connor's body had aged from years of hard work, she had no regrets for herself. She enjoyed pampering Mrs. Rowan and even excused her for not having any domestic skills. Mrs. Rowan is seen as a delicate flower; on the other hand, when Peggy revealed that she could not sew, the other Irish women looked at her in disbelief.

The realization that she was different from the Rowans was brought home more forcibly to Peggy when she tried to take a bath in the bathroom. Mrs. Madden, the housekeeper, angrily told Peggy, "You will not dare to wash yourself there" (123). Peggy was good enough to scrub and clean for the Rowans' family but she was certainly not good enough to bathe in the same bath they do. She was a servant, not a part of the honored family.

Summary of Race and Class Representations in **Wildflower Girl.** In this novel racial issues center around the Irish immigrant's yearning to be like the American women. Their features were so soft and they looked delicate, while the Irish women were rough and beaten by years of hard work. I took the appearances of the women as a racial issue because many instances of discrimination against different groups have dealt with how they looked, based on their ethnic and regional origin.

Peggy was reminded that she was from a different socioeconomic class. She could not let her dreams for the future be known. Her sole purpose was to ensure that the rich continued to live in luxurious comfort. The Irish women cooked, cleaned, sewed, and did everything for the rich but they had to keep their dreams on hold. They were not of the same socioeconomic caliber as the "Americans" they labored for.

The Slave Dancer by Paula Fox (1973)

***Race Representations in* The Slave Dancer.** Race plays a major role in this novel, more explicitly so than in the other novels in this period. This book portrays a total disregard for other human lives, all because one group of people believe that they are superior to all other human beings. Although the story is focused on the experiences of a young white boy called Jessie, through his story we see the Africans who were being brought to the West as slaves. We see the subhuman conditions these "soon to be slaves" had to survive before they were brought to the United States and sold into slavery, a further degradation of their humanity. On the ship, Jessie soon discovered that the captain treated more than his "African gold" cargo with contempt.

The captain regarded himself as an American and showed his intolerance for others. He had little respect for the French and Irish. He told Jessie, "Bad fellows, the French….Pirates all of them" (20). He called one of his seasoned sailors a "scoundrel" and an "Irish bucket" (45). The captain was very quick to judge other people but did not see evil in himself and in the slave trade he so zealously carried on.

The other crewmen also demonstrated what little regard they had for the Africans. They saw their job as a money-making venture and cared nothing about whom they would hurt in the process. They declared the slave trade to be "black gold" (29) and insisted that the native chiefs were so greedy that they sold their people for cheap trading goods.

They felt justified in their trade, since they could pass some of the blame to the African leaders. Simply, if the leaders did not care for their own people, why should they? They were also angry at the English, who now want to stop them from making their fortunes in the slave trade. After all, the English started the slave trade but now they were acting as if they were on the side of the slaves.

When the captain's mate in a drunken stupor shot an African captive, the captain ordered the others to throw the mate overboard. Again, his total disregard for others comes across. Regardless of who you were, if you got in the captain's way, you would regret it. He had no regard for the Africans other than the profit he could make off their heads. And he had even less regard for his crewmen.

The final analysis of racial issues in the novel was one that was very obvious throughout the whole story. There are at least twelve instances of the word "nigger" in the novel. The frequent usage of the word serves as a very disturbing reminder of how a negative label can be used to hurt others. The word can also be deemed a stereotypical identification.

Class Representations in The Slave Dancer. It is arguable that the socioeconomic status of Jessie's family had a major impact on the horrendous experience he had being captured and taken away on a slave ship where he was forced to play his fife, and on the ordeal he endured as he was being ill-treated and witnessed hundreds of Africans being ill-treated too.

Jessie lived with his mother and sister in a one-room home that also doubled as his mother's sewing room. The sparseness of the room explains the reasons Jessie's mother worked all day as a seamstress to take care of her two children. The family had barely any possessions at all; thus Jessie daydreams of a better life and a better day.

Amid his dreams, however, he was brought back to the reality of where he lived. He was being kidnapped to be taken aboard the slaver. Immediately his dreams were suspended as he fought for his freedom.

As a member of the ship's crew, Jessie again came to understand the differences in how the crew members were treated. All the crewmen were given rations for eating and drinking. However, this ration did not apply to the captain. One of the crewmen told Jessie that "captain of this ship would drink your blood before he'd go without" (31). While the crewmen ate stale bread and had to limit the amount of water they drank, the captain fed on fresh chicken, eggs, and vegetables, delicacies he reserved for himself.

Summary of Race and Class Representations in The Slave Dancer.
Race is clearly evident, from the way the captain treated his crewmen to
the way they in turn treated the slaves. Purvis, the Irish crewman, got
angry that people showed feelings for the slaves when his people had
suffered grave injustice at the hand of other whites years before. The
captain enjoyed hurling racial slurs at the crewmen. The slaves were
treated as commodities and not as people. They were simply "black
gold" and the crew and captain's only concern with them is that they
stay alive until they were sold.

Class representation demonstrates that with the way the blacks are
treated, it is better to be poor and hungry than to be black. Also, the captain's attitude demonstrates that people in authority look out for their
needs before they consider the needs of those of lower socioeconomic
status than themselves.

Sing Down the Moon by Scott O'Dell (1970)

Race Representations in Sing Down the Moon. The issues of race are
evident in the treatment of the Navaho tribe and other Native Americans
at the hands of the white settlers. Bright Morning's life at home was
normal and peaceful until the white settlers arrived. She tended her
mother's sheep and enjoyed time with her best friend.

The white soldiers watched the Navahos' every move and decided
what they could and could not do. It is ironic that while these soldiers or
"Long Knives" determined that the Navahos could not go on fighting
with other tribes, they felt they had the freedom to kill the Navahos if
they disobeyed the soldiers.

When Bright Morning was captured and sold into slavery, the white
mistress complained about her attitude and her features. Bright Morning
walked "pigeon-toed" (35) and did not smile. The woman claimed that
the Hopis did not walk pigeon-toed; thus, she wanted a slave from this
tribe. The Spanish slaver promised to find her one in the fall.

Bright Morning is supposed to appear cheerful when in fact she is
being sold into slavery. Her feelings are obviously not important, as the
mistress and the slaver communicate in front of her. She is further
described as a "strong" girl who is also a "hard" worker. The transaction
is depicted as a sale of livestock.

Shortly after Bright Morning escaped and returned home, the Long Knives came in and relocated the tribe to a settlement camp. The settlers were determined that the decisions they made for the Navahos would be carried out. As the tribe succumbed to its fate and was forced to walk many miles to the resettlement area, it realized the extent of its captivity.

Showing their superiority to the Native Americans, the settlers kept a close watch over them, keeping them from communication with other tribes also in captivity. They even monitored the Native Americans' rations, forcing them to eat flour made of wheat and drink water from the muddy river. They had never had flour before and many became ill. Also, the water from the river was bitter. The Native Americans, who once were independent people, were now forced to depend on the white settlers for their very existence.

***Class Representations in* Sing Down the Moon.** Before their forced migration, the economic status of families within the tribe could be determined by how many heads of sheep they had. Bright Morning's father was a leader in the tribe and her mother owned one of the largest flocks of sheep. This made Bright Morning a very desirable bridal candidate for one of the tribe's young warriors. Bright Morning was not pretty but she would make a good wife since she could weave well and knew how to tend the sheep. Because of her mother's status in the tribe, she would get a good husband because every mother tried to make sure her son married someone with wealth (large flocks of sheep).

Looking back at her experiences of being sold into slavery, Bright Morning came to understand why the young slave girl, Rosita, at her mistress's house did not want to run away too. Rosita came from a poor family within her tribe, and she liked the food and clothes the mistress bought her. She also got to sleep in a soft bed and had a big room to herself (43). Life as a slave was much better than being with her own people.

***Summary of Race and Class Representations in* Sing Down the Moon.** Racism is brought out in the inhumane way in which the Navahos were treated. The white settlers felt they had a legal right to dictate the every move of the tribe while the tribe had no input in their own lives. Their eating habits were forcibly changed, and they were marched out of their homes and taken to areas where the tribes had to be dependent on the settlers for everything.

Class issues were brought out in the strained relationship between the Navahos and the Apaches. Class is also evident in the way the white soldiers, overnight, destroyed everything the Navahos owned, fields and cattle, and forced them into a dependency state. People who fought their own battles and supported their families now had to wait to be told what and when to eat.

Combined Analysis of the Novels
in the Early Immigration Wave: 1820–1899

This section of the analysis deals with the collective critique of the four novels in the early immigration wave, incorporating the subquestions of the four questions guiding the study. It also incorporates the historical data for this period, looking particularly at how historical issues relate to or inform the issues of race and class that were analyzed in the novels.

What Are the Common Images of Immigrants in Children's Literature?

The first question of this analysis is used to explore the common representational images of immigrants in the novels being analyzed. The broader issue of representation was broken into smaller units to look specifically at who the immigrants of the early wave were, where they immigrated from, and their experiences before and after they arrived.

Who Are the Immigrants?

Of the four novels, three of the protagonists are females: Antonia in *My Antonia*; Peggy in *Wildflower Girl*; and Bright Morning in *Sing Down the Moon*. The fourth protagonist is Jessie, the young boy in *The Slave Dancer*. Bright Morning's character is the only one who does not reflect a recent immigrant story in the sense being discussed in this research: travelers from one country to another. It is important, however, in that the Native Americans' experience played a major role in the early immigration wave.

Where Do They Come From?

The novels represent people from different nations. Antonia Shimerda and her family in *My Antonia* immigrated from Bohemia and settled in Nebraska hoping to make a comfortable life as homesteaders. Peggy O'Driscoll in *Wildflower Girl* came from Ireland, at the height of the Great Potato Famine, to find her fortune. Jessie in *The Slave Dancer* was born in Louisiana but his father's family came from France in earlier settlement periods. Finally, Bright Morning in *Sing Down the Moon* came from Arizona where her tribe, the Navahos, made their home before forced resettlement.

What Are Their Experiences Before and After They Came?

Before Experiences. The before experiences portrayed in the novels are mixed. In *My Antonia,* the Shimerdas relate that they were respectable people in their country and that they came looking for a more prosperous life. Unlike many other families who traveled alone and then worked to send for other family members, as was the common practice during this immigration period, the entire family came together.

In *Wildflower Girl*, Peggy's life just before immigrating was filled with poverty and loss. Her family struggled to hold onto their pastry shop until the landlord's decision to sell forced them to close down. Like many young girls during this period, Peggy traveled to America alone, hoping to find a job so she could send money home to her family.

In *The Slave Dancer*, Jessie's early experiences also portray a poor beginning. Living in a one-room apartment, his mother struggled to support the family after her husband's death. Jessie tried to contribute to the family's income by playing his fife on the docks, hoping he would be rewarded for his services.

In *Sing Down the Moon*, Bright Morning's life before the white settlers arrived seemed peaceful. Her father was a leader of the tribe and her mother owned many sheep. This gave the family a respected status in the community.

After Experiences. Various occurrences helped to shape the later experiences in the lives of the four protagonists. Although their experiences changed dramatically for the worse, for the most part, they all

share something in common. They were each able to reminisce pos-
itively on earlier experiences in their lives.

After arriving in Nebraska, the Shimerdas suffered many major
setbacks. They bought a farm from a fellow Bohemian who charged
them more than the fair price; the "house" was a dugout in the ground.
They were unprepared for the harsh winter, so the whole family had to
share one winter coat. They could not communicate in English so they had to
depend on Krajiek, the fellow Bohemian, who did not have their best
interests at heart. Unable to bear the new life, Mr. Shimerda committed
suicide, creating further distress for the family. Soon, with the help of
the townspeople the family was able to make a new start, plant their own
crops, raise their own animals, and build a better house. Antonia's life
changed from being pampered by her loving father to being a farmhand,
then a cook, and eventually to raising a large family of her own. As a
young lady, jilted by her fiancé, Antonia returned home pregnant and
alone. Everyone felt her life was over. However, she met and married a
Bohemian immigrant and her life, though filled with many children and
hard work, turned out well. Antonia credits her cultural exposure with
her ability to take good care of her children and to see to it that they
were never hired out to anyone.

Peggy, in *Wildflower Girl*, got a job fulfilling her wishes of being of
service. Life for her, however, was not as easy. Because Peggy was able
to read, she had a likely chance of succeeding in her new homeland. This
gave her the opportunity to dream of the future. Peggy learned to think
toward the future, she saved and sent home money to help her family,
and she determines that she is in America to stay.

In *The Slave Dancer* Jessie came to realize that his humble home was
better when compared to life on the ship. He learned the truth firsthand
about how slaves were treated when they were brought to America. For
the first time, he learned the meaning of racial prejudice as the captain
disrespected anyone he felt was not an "American."

In *Sing Down the Moon* Bright Morning and her tribe's experiences
changed from pure contentment to bondage. They could no longer plant
crops and herd their own animals because the white settlers destroyed
everything they had. They were uprooted and taken to a resettlement
camp. With the same determination she had exhibited when she escaped
from being sold into slavery, Bright Morning escaped the resettlement
camp with her husband and returned to the land she called home.

The experiences of the characters in the novel affirm the historical presentation at the beginning of this chapter. All remain poor but some are better off than others. The white immigrants' lives are better than those of the nonwhites. Bright Morning (the Native American) is back on the run but her freedom is at best uncertain. As for the white immigrants, Antonia becomes a mother of many children but she and her husband own a huge farm and are able to provide for them. Peggy's dreams of a better life in America imply that all will be well. Her hopes are validated when the head housekeeper, who is also Irish, leaves to open her own boarding house. Finally, Jessie returns home to his mother and sister, learns a trade, and later takes the family out of poverty.

How Are Issues of Race and Class Represented in the Novels?

The critique of race and class representations conducted in the analysis of the early immigration wave novels speaks specifically to the main and subquestions for this section.

How Are Characters Racially Identified?

The protagonists in the early immigration novels, all white except for Bright Morning, the Navaho girl, are considered outsiders. Like the immigrants of the early wave who were distinguished by where they came from, the characters in the novels are racially identified according to their place of origin.

Are Issues of Race and Class Present in the Novels?

The issues of race and class have been discussed at length at the beginning of the analytic process. This was done because I wanted to give precedence to the topics this study was intended to look at in-depth. I combined the two questions (Are there issues of race and class? and How are these issues handled?) because I felt that both questions are closely linked in this section of the discussion.

Several instances of race and class representations of immigrants were identified in all four novels. Each book addressed different aspects of race and class according to the context of each story. In *My Antonia*, the negative racial representation of the immigrants is very visible. Characters who are not "Americans" all seem to have some distinguishing characteristics that make them peculiar, like the Russian men Pavel and Peter. Their class status is also evident. Although some of the young immigrant girls had very successful lives, they were still the outsiders. They were not the girls the "American" boys would marry, and although they had money (Lena was a successful dressmaker and Tiny a very rich entrepreneur), they still remained outsiders. Antonia, the star immigrant in the story, ended up back on a farm with a large family, her children speaking Bohemian exclusively until they went to school where they were taught English. This ending scenario puts the immigrants' experience in perspective. Regardless of the American exposure, they are still immigrants. Their lives ultimately turn out differently from those of "Americans."

In *Wildflower Girl*, Peggy is overwhelmed with the beauty of the "other." She is portrayed as an Irish immigrant who has never seen beautiful women before she came to America. Racism is brought to the fore in the comparative image of the American woman as a delicate being and the Irish woman as a hardworking domestic whose main job is to help the American woman maintain her delicacy. Class representations are also negative. The Irish woman must stifle her dreams because she is "intended" to be a hard worker. Peggy could admire the rich family's home and gardens but she could not let them know this. She broke from this mold when the housekeeper, who had saved up her money, went away to open a business of her own. Peggy realized the strength in her silence. She wanted to be more than a housemaid, and knew that if she kept dreaming about a better life she could make it a reality.

In *The Slave Dancer* Jessie realized firsthand how people of different racial backgrounds are treated. Racism is present in the way the captain treated him because he was of French descent, the way Purvis ("the Irish bucket") was treated because of his Irish origin, and the inhumane way the Africans were treated like trading goods. Class representations rest on the treatment of crew members by the captain. The captain set strict limits for them but allowed himself to splurge by saving particular delicacies for himself. Jessie was reminded that he should be happy with his position and color. His life could be worse; it could be comparable to that of the slaves.

Finally, in *Sing Down the Moon,* racism is obvious in the treatment of the Native Americans by the white settlers. The Native Americans were driven from their homes to concentrated areas where they lost their weapons and, therefore, their power to fight the enemy. They were not members of the now "ruling class" or the "white Anglo-Saxon Protestants" thus their first settlers' claim to American territory was blatantly disregarded. Class representations stand out in the way different tribes were pitted against each other. The Apaches were given special treatment, being fed before all others. In spite of this preferential treatment, they continued to fight against the Navaho tribesmen. This reaction, however, indicates that the tribes did not consider themselves to be "one." Each tribe fought to keep its individuality in spite of the demeaning way each was being treated by the white settlers.

Do These Images Change for Different Immigrant Groups?

The negative images that are presented about the different immigrant groups are common across the four novels. If characters were immigrants, there was always something about them that justified their being "different"; for example, the immigrant would frequently be preoccupied with wanting to change his or her physical features. Although the stories were different, the treatment of immigrants is the same in the sense that they were overwhelmingly the "outsiders" or the "others."

How Are Different Immigrant Groups Presented?

The different immigrant groups in the novels are presented differently. Individuals may be resourceful but groups are not treated equally. Although the stories seem well intentioned in that they look at the experiences of immigrant folks, the way the immigrants are portrayed usually comes across negatively. For example, the Shimerdas spoke little English, so this caused them to be cheated by none other than a fellow Bohemian. Their misplaced distrust of Austrians indicates that if they were more trusting of others they could have been told that they were being cheated. As a newly arrived Irish immigrant, Peggy had to work to support herself. She was not allowed to openly envision herself in a "prosperous" house. She must be content to be a housemaid. Jessie was a

poor boy dressed in rags, thus, he justifiably becomes the kidnapping
target for sailors working on a slave boat bound for Africa. And Bright
Morning's tribe, the Navaho, lost all sense of self-governance when they
were marched for miles on end to a resettlement camp, where the white
settlers in essence incarcerate them.

How Do Characters Handle Cross-Cultural Encounters?

Each character deals with cross-cultural interactions differently. Antonia
welcomed her friendship with Jim and excitedly took pleasure in
learning American customs and in teaching Jim about her Bohemian
customs. Peggy was disappointed by her initial encounters in America
and dreamed of going back home. However, realizing that there were
many opportunities for her in America, she conceded that she was
"home" and determined to better herself. Learning the new culture while
leaning on her Irish culture, she would survive. Jessie befriended Ras, a
young African boy among the slaves being shipped back to the West.
When the ship went down in a fight with a British ship, the two boys were
the only survivors. They taught each other words from their respective
languages, and Jessie came to befriend a black person for the first time.
For Bright Morning, however, her cross-cultural interactions did not
prove successful. She escaped from cross-cultural encounters twice:
once after being sold into slavery, and again from the resettlement camp
back to the land she grew up on.

Historical Evaluation of Early Immigration Novels

Although the novels exhibited many instances where the issues of race
and class presented a negative representation of immigrants in the early
immigration period, the negative treatment seems consistent with the
way immigrants of the period were treated. Of course much of this
understanding of the historical data discussed at the beginning of the
chapter was gleaned not from the common history as told about the
making of the United States of America but from delving into alternative
historical recordings that gave voice to the underrepresented groups of
the time (for example, the Irish immigrants).

Antonia, Peggy, Jessie, and Bright Morning are each presented as hardworking individuals who care about the welfare of their families. They work and suffer because of their families but think highly of where they came from. The immigrants of the early immigration period had strong family ties. Everyone was responsible for helping in the family; the family was usually concerned with doing what was best for one another, going out and finding jobs to supplement the parents' incomes and blending the exposures to their new cultures with the experiences they brought from their own cultures. Each of the main characters in the four novels displayed many of these characteristics. The father figure was absent from the families of Antonia, Peggy, and Jessie. This absence indicated that the families had a higher degree of difficulty in trying to survive financially. No father figure meant certain poverty. Certain poverty meant that they would indeed be dependent on the government for support.

Antonia's experience as an immigrant who spoke no English is consistent with the historical data in the way she learned the language and then taught it to the other members of her family. Peggy knew the language but was initially an outsider because of her ethnic origin. She stood ahead of the crowd in that not only did she speak English, she was able to read and write it too. This, along with her determination to make something of herself, presents some hope that she would succeed. In the early immigration wave many immigrants could not read and write; thus, it was difficult for them as they tried to upgrade their socioeconomic status. Jessie also knew the language, but he was initially disenchanted with the poor way his family lived. After his horrendous journey at sea, he was happy to return home to his meager beginnings. His experiences helped to shape what he would later become as an adult. Bright Morning, however, refused to conform to the life others planned for her. She was determined to live the life her family had originally provided for her. Native American tribes were historically mistreated in that they would lose their land whenever immigration numbers increased and the white settlers needed more land to expand their growing frontier. Bright Morning's strong resistance seems plausible. She proved to be a fighter, fighting back at every chance.

Many early immigrants who were not "white Anglo-Saxon Protestants" had to undergo many demeaning experiences to be accepted in American society. They suffered because of the way they looked, the way they spoke, and where they lived when they arrived in the United

States. With no exception, these four characters displayed strong individual characteristics that shaped their destinies and helped to identify them as part of the early wave of immigrants. Their experiences give us a sense of the real experiences of regular immigrants and how those experiences fit with the historical recordings of these people's experiences. Indeed, the stories ascertain that we take a more critical look at our understandings of immigrants in this period.

Chapter 4

The Middle Immigration Wave: 1900–1964

The middle immigration period, which spans the years from 1900 to 1964, realized a demographic change in the nationalities of immigrants who came to the United States. A large number of immigrants in this wave came between 1900 and 1920 and consisted of people from central, eastern, and southern Europe (Banks 1997; Easterlin et al. 1982; Kellogg 1988). They emigrated from countries such as Italy, Hungary, Poland, and Russia. Many spoke no English, came from rural areas, and were Catholic (Kellogg 1988).

As these newcomers' numbers increased, people sought to distinguish them from earlier waves of immigrants who came from the northern and western parts of Europe (Banks 1997). They became the "new" immigrants, and the early wave immigrants became the "old" immigrants. Banks further notes that the new immigrants were deemed inferior to the early wave immigrants. Their increase was blamed on steamship companies and American industries, which needed unskilled workers to fulfill their labor demands.

The Dillingham Commission, formed in 1907 to investigate trends in immigration, concluded that there was a "fundamental difference in both the character and the causes of the new and old immigrations" (Banks 1997: 267). Nativists pressed the government to take stricter measures to curb the influx of the new wave.

Based on the Dillingham Commission's findings, a series of "severely restrictive statutes" were enacted to limit the rapid increase in this new wave of immigrants (Easterlin et al. 1982: 94). The Immigration Act of 1917, the first of many to follow, put in place a literacy test for all new immigrants over the age of sixteen. Those who failed the test were refused admittance into the country. As the immigration numbers continued to increase, the nativists demanded even tighter eliminating measures. The Johnson Act of 1921 marked a turning point in American history (Banks 1997). This act set a national quota system that imposed the first numerical limits on European immigrants.

Immigrants could enter the United States based on the percentage of a particular country's immigrants already living here. Since the majority of immigrants were from northern and western Europe, these countries benefited tremendously. The 1924 Johnson-Reed Act established more extreme national quotas, adding a clause prohibiting the immigration of anyone ineligible for citizenship. This literally stopped Asian immigration (Banks 1997). The act proved a triumph for the nativists and resulted in a dramatic decrease in immigrants coming from eastern and southern Europe.

The Great Depression of the 1930s, strengthened by the very restrictive national quotas, effectuated a decrease in the number of immigrants entering the United States (Kellogg 1988). This period brought the smallest number of immigrants since the 1830s, and for the first time the number of people leaving the United States exceeded the number entering (Easterlin et al. 1982). As war raged in various countries in Europe, however, the immigration laws were challenged. The federal government sought to give refuge to millions of people driven from their homelands. The 1940 Displaced Persons Act provided admission for refugees to settle permanently over a two-year period. Preference was given to people from the Baltic states. Jewish and Catholic refugees from Poland who came after this date were largely excluded from the provisions of the Displaced Persons Act.

While the Displaced Persons Act allowed refugees to enter, it was very restrictive. Refugees were not allowed to enter as "nonquota" immigrants; thus it set a limit on the number of people who could immigrate. A revision of the act was passed in 1950, liberalizing the terms for admission and increasing the annual quotas (Easterlin et al. 1982). The Baltic preference provision was removed and provisions that discriminated against the Polish Jews and Catholics were eliminated. Other refugee acts followed, providing asylum for people of different countries threatened by Communist rule. While the 1952 McCarran-Walter Immigration Act preserved the national quota system established by the 1924 Johnson-Reed Act, it dropped the Asian exclusion clause and granted Asian Americans naturalization rights. Thus, Korean refugees were granted asylum. The Refugee Relief Act of 1953 admitted 205,000 immigrants as nonquota immigrants. The 1956 Act suspended the annual quota for refugees and allowed 20,000 refugees from Hungary, China, and Yugoslavia to immigrate. The 1960 World Refugee

Year Law brought in immigrants from Cuba and China. These acts set precedents for refugees from southeast Asia (Easterlin et al. 1982).

Who Are They?: People in the Middle Immigration Wave

While there are many groups that have contributed to the makeup of the immigrants of the middle wave, the remainder of this section focuses on those groups reflected in the middle immigration wave novels: Jewish, Polish, Ukrainian, and Chinese immigrants. Like the immigrants in the early wave, many of these people came to improve their economic condition and to seek religious and political freedom (Banks 1997). However, because many came from different geographical areas, they were openly discriminated against by immigrants already living in the United States.

The Jews in the Middle Immigration Wave

Jewish Americans have immigrated from every country in Europe and from all over the world (Brownstone 1988b). Much of their history has been marked by oppression. Like many other groups of immigrants, the Jewish-American presence in the United States dates back to the earliest discoveries of North America. The earliest Jews to reach America arrived with Christopher Columbus in 1492 (Banks 1997; Brownstone 1988b).

Between 1881 and 1924 more than two million Jews emigrated from eastern Europe because of "anti-Jewish legislation and pogroms (govern-ment-sponsored attacks) against them" (Banks 1997: 306). This discussion of Jewish-American immigrants centers on those from Russia and Germany. The majority of these people immigrated in search of religious freedom because Nazi factions deprived them of this free existence in their homelands.

Many middle wave immigrants settled in northeastern cities, par-ticularly New York, Boston, Philadelphia, and Baltimore. They moved into densely populated ethnic neighborhoods, where many found work in the clothing industry. Working conditions were often deplorable. Many immigrants worked long hours in sweatshop environments seven days a week in order to meet unreasonable deadlines. Takaki (1993) asserts that the treatment of these garment workers was comparable to the experiences of blacks in America.

Some immigrants also became peddlers. By 1906, Jewish peddlers made up over fifty percent of peddlers in New York. The Jewish peddler later became a figure of Jewish-American folklore (Takaki 1993). By 1910, over seventy percent of Jewish daughters worked to help support their families. They made up over one-third of the garment industry's work force. The 1924 Johnson-Reed Act proved a major barrier for many Jewish immigrants fleeing persecution, because the act pointedly limited the immigration of eastern Europeans.

The period between 1930 and 1940 marked a very difficult period for Jews in the United States. Anti-Semitism, fueled by Nazi propaganda, reached an intolerable level (Banks 1997). Jewish Americans were discriminated against in certain professions and occupations, and they were excluded from residential areas, social clubs, resorts, private schools, and universities (Banks 1997). While the 1948 Displaced Persons Act blatantly discriminated against further Jewish immigration, the 1950 revised act opened the doors, once again, for those who were tragic refugees from the Nazi persecution.

Takaki (1993) maintains that Jewish Americans worked hard at becoming more "American." Their main goal was not to be seen by others as a "greenhorn." A greenhorn was an individual who had just arrived in the United States and had not yet become accustomed to the American lifestyle.

Education became a sure means of social and economic improvement. Language was also very important. Many eagerly learned English so they could "become 'regular Yankees' and lessen the ethnic distance between them and native-born Americans" (Takaki 1993: 299). As the assimilation process progressed, many anglicized their names. By the 1940s, Jewish Americans moved from a working-class to a middle-class community, establishing phenomenal records of achievement.

The Poles in the Middle Immigration Wave

Polish Americans have been making the United States their home for many years. The ethnic community is normally referred to as "Polonia" (Lopata 1994). Historically besieged by bordering countries for example Germany and Russia, Polish residents have often had to seek political asylum in the United States. Many who came between 1900 and 1920 did so mainly for economic reasons, while immigrants in later years came for political and religious reasons (Lopata 1994). Immigrants in the earlier part of this period numbered nearly two million (Wytrwal 1969). Jewish immigrants were a large part of this group. Others were predominantly Catholics. When they arrived, they settled in northern states where other Polish populations were established.

Polish Americans in the middle immigration wave were very actively supportive of their homeland. During World War I, many were among the first volunteers to fight in the American Army, helping Poland to gain its freedom from Germany (Wytrwal 1969). Wytrwal further notes that although they only made up four percent of the American population, Polish Americans accounted for twelve percent of World War I casualties. Many also fought for Poland's independence during World War II.

The Displaced Persons Acts of 1948 and 1950 helped many Polish immigrants to find refuge in America. Many who sought asylum during World War II had been placed in concentration or labor camps in Germany (Lopata 1994). Unwilling to return to their communist-controlled homeland, they were determined to succeed in the United States. The Poles in America still maintain many of their customs (Nowakowski 1989), although they have widely assimilated into American customs.

The Ukrainians in the Middle Immigration Wave

The Ukrainian-American community is regarded as one of the best organized ethnic groups in America (Kuropas 1972). While Ukrainian immigrants started immigrating in 1865, most came between 1870 and 1914. Some were recorded as Poles, Slovaks, Russians, and Hungarians by the Census Bureau. Kuropas (1972) establishes that early immigrants in this period were peasant farmers. Since industry was limited, jobs were scarce. Taxes were high and poverty was a constant companion. Many sold their lands and borrowed money from relatives in order to emigrate. When they arrived in America, eighty-five percent settled in Pennsylvania, New York, and New Jersey. Most became miners in the anthracite coal countries of Pennsylvania. Working conditions were deplorable and there was a high rate of lung cancer. Since they had no unions, the miners were essentially at the mercy of their employers.

The dream of a better life was never realized for many immigrants, as they toiled hard for very little money to support their families. Those who settled in industrial cities also worked long hours but their lives were in less danger. Many came expecting to have their own farms but realized that the cost of land was more than they could afford. Immigration for many peasants decreased between 1920 and 1930 because of the laws restricting immigrants from southern and eastern Europe.

After World War II, however, Ukrainian immigrants refusing to return to Russian dictatorship were permitted to enter under the 1948 Displaced Persons Act. While many of the earlier immigrants had very limited education and came mainly to escape poverty, many of the political refugees of the 1940s were better educated. Many of these immigrants had at least an eighth-grade education, with others being college graduates and professionals.

Many members of the Ukrainian community have worked hard to dually maintain their heritage and help others assimilate into American society. Kuropas (1972) posits that Ukrainian immigrants have "adapted to the American way of life" and have been "loyal and patriotic" (65). The Ukrainian National Association encourages them to become American citizens so they can participate fully in every facet of American life.

The Chinese in the Middle Immigration Wave

The middle immigration wave had a mixed effect on Chinese immigration. After the 1882 Chinese Exclusion Act took effect, Chinese immigration was totally eliminated. The negative treatment of the Chinese as the "yellow peril" (Wu 1982) prompted many to return to China. In 1890 there were over 100,000 Chinese immigrants, but by 1920 only half of that number remained (Brownstone 1988a). Those who stayed, changed their work style. Many went into service occupations—small businesses that were traditionally laundries and restaurants—and others went into domestic work. In essence they did jobs that other Americans would not do. As anti-Chinese sentiments increased, the Chinese immigrants became more united. The "Chinatowns" became more of a haven. However, Chinese Americans resisted their exclusion in every way they could. They did not just sit around and accept their fate (Brownstone 1988a).

After the 1911 revolution in China, some Chinese Americans went back home to help rebuild their homeland. Most stayed, however, and began to build the Chinese-American community (Brownstone 1988a). The long process of becoming "more American" began for those who stayed behind. As the Chinese immigrants became more American, several changes took effect. Their traditional Chinese dress was one of the first customs to go. The men cut off their queues and wore their hair American-style. Soon, women began moving into professions as equals. The Chinese Americans soon started wearing American clothes, learning to speak English well, and building their own social organizations. They aligned themselves and built political strength (Brownstone 1988a).

The year 1949 marked an important year for some Chinese Americans. Many students who were studying here stayed after Communist factions took over China. This marked a turning point in Chinese-American history. These people soon adopted mainstream American lifestyles and lived in high-income mixed communities. As the 1952 immigration laws ended the exclusion of Chinese immigrants, more started to arrive. Family members left behind in China were now able to reunite. As they became adapted to their new homeland, these immigrants have presented a united ethnic front, helping others to immigrate and establish successful business communities. After overcoming decades of overt discrimination, the Chinese-American community is now one of the fastest-growing immigrant groups in the United States.

Novels in the Middle Immigration Wave: 1900–1964

The eight middle immigration wave novels are *Letters from Rifka* (Hesse 1992), *Journey to America* (Levitin 1970), *Silver Days* (Levitin 1989), *The Cat Who Escaped from Steerage* (Mayerson 1990), *Land of Hope* (Nixon 1992); *Good-bye to the Trees* (Shiefman 1993), *Good-bye Billy Radish* (Skurzynski 1992), and *The Star Fisher* (Yep 1991). They relate tales of immigrant children from Russia, Germany, Poland, Ukraine, and China. Each novel contributes important insights into the middle immigrant experiences. Five of the novels in this immigrant wave relate tales of Jewish immigrant experiences. Only one novel relates a nonwhite experience.

Synopses of the Middle Immigrant Novels

Hesse, Karen. (1992). *Letters from Rifka.* New York: Trumpet Club. 148 pp.

   Letters from Rifka tells the compelling story of a young Jewish girl, Rifka, and her family's journey from Russia to the United States in 1919. After surviving racial and religious persecution in their homeland, the family is smuggled into Poland, where they make arrangements for the journey to America. On the day they are scheduled to leave, they discover that Rifka has ringworm, so she has to stay behind. Rifka suffers many other obstacles as she waits to join the rest of her family in America.

Levitin, Sonia. (1970). *Journey to America.* New York: Aladdin. 150 pp.

   Journey to America relates the experiences of a Jewish family, the Platts, fleeing Germany in 1938. The father escapes first and then, after his family manages to travel into Switzerland, he sends for them to join him in America. While they wait to join him, however, Mrs. Platt and the children suffer many hardships and struggle to stay together. Eventually, Mr. Platt saves enough money to pay their passage to America.

Levitin, Sonia. (1989). *Silver Days.* New York: Aladdin. 186 pp.

   The sequel to *Journey to America*, this story highlights the Platt family's experiences after their arrival in America. Told through the eyes of thirteen-year-old Lisa, we see the many struggles the family faces as they move from New York to California. Eventually, the family rises above these humble beginnings.

Mayerson, Evelyn W. (1990). *The Cat Who Escaped from Steerage.* New York: Macmillan. 66 pp.

   Nine-year-old Chanah travels with her Polish family to live in America. They are packed together with hundreds of other immigrants in steerage. When Chanah's stray cat (which she rescued and smuggled on board) escapes, she and her cousin secretly search the ship. As their search takes them to different levels of the ship, they discover that not everyone travels to America in steerage.

Nixon, Joan L. (1992). *Land of Hope*. New York: Bantam Doubleday Dell. 171 pp.

Young Rebekah Levinsky and her Russian family immigrate to America in 1902 in search of a better life. Rebekah dreams of attending college and getting an education, something unheard of in her old country. The family is forced to work in her uncle's sweatshop and Rebekah almost abandons her dreams as she helps her parents.

Shiefman, Vicky. (1993). *Good-bye to the Trees*. New York: Macmillan. 150 pp.

Thirteen-year-old Fagel Fratrizsky is chosen by her mother to travel from Russia to America for a better life in 1907. Fagel arrives in Massachusetts with hopes of working hard to bring the rest of her family to America. She demonstrates courage and determination as she insists on learning English, saves money to send for one brother, and walks away from her job after her employer steals some of her savings.

Skurzynski, Gloria. (1992). *Good-bye Billy Radish*. New York: Aladdin. 137 pp.

Good-bye Billy Radish relates a powerful story of friendship between an "American" boy named Hank and a Ukrainian immigrant named Bazyli, "Billy." Through Hank's eyes we see the pleasures and heartaches of two friends, growing up in 1917, as they come to grips with who they are and what is expected of them as they mature, working in the steel mills.

Yep, Laurence. (1991). *The Star Fisher*. New York: Puffin. 150 pp.

In 1927, Joan Lee and her family move from Ohio to West Virginia, hoping to open a laundry and start new lives. However, the Lees, who are the first Chinese Americans to move into town, face racial discrimination from the outset. With the help of their landlord, Miss Lucy, the family is slowly accepted by the community. Soon, the townspeople begin to patronize the Lees' laundry and everyone loves Mrs. Lee's famous apple pies.

Individual Analysis of the Middle Immigrant Novels

Letters from Rifka by Karen Hesse (1992)

Race Representations in Letters from Rifka. As Rifka and her family waited in hiding to get out of Russia, Rifka became the family's decoy for the soldiers. The Jews were hated not because they were a threat to the well-being of the country, but simply because of who they were. Rifka was saddened by the way the soldiers berated her family as they searched the train to see if her family was hiding under the cargo. The soldiers passed judgment without knowing who her family really were. Rifka knew the Jews were being used to fuel hatred among the Russian citizens in order to divert attention from the real economic and political troubles the country was having.

The family knew that in order to divert attention from their hiding places they needed Rifka. She could be considered a Russian peasant instead of a Jewish girl because of her physical features. Captivated by her beautiful blond hair, one of the guards forgot his mission and came over to flirt with her. Her ploy worked until her uncle, who was highly esteemed as a businessman, came running with the news that his place of business had been robbed. This was his ruse to further protect his brother's family. The soldiers reluctantly left to investigate his claims. Rifka realized how easily an individual's appearance could aid or betray them.

Rifka was finally able to come to America after months of therapy in Belgium to cure her ringworm disease. However, she was detained at Ellis Island because her hair had not regrown. The family anxiously hoped and prayed that she would not be counted among the "undesirables" whom America would not allow to immigrate. At the detaining center, Rifka quickly learned English and was able to interpret several languages for the doctors and nurses. While everyone was amazed with her remarkable ability to learn languages quickly, they still worried that she would not be able to marry, and feared that she would become a ward of the government.

While her fate was uncertain, Rifka still reached out to help someone else, a young Russian boy, and save him from being sent back to Russia. She didn't let the Russians' hatred of Jews stand in the way of her helping a non-Jewish Russian citizen.

***Class Representations in* Letters from Rifka.** In Russia, Jewish families (particularly those who had no political or business advantage) were forced to keep only two of any item in their houses. They could be punished for disobeying these direct orders. Rifka marveled that her uncle's house was not searched because of his status. She mused in a letter to her cousin, "In your house there are many fine things, Tovah, but they never inspected your house" (31).

As Rifka prepared to leave Belgium for America, the representative from the Hebrew Immigrant Aid Society advised her to travel on a small boat because on the ship "rich people...travel in first class or second class, but the poor people travel in steerage" (72–73). She was able to travel on the small ship because she saved everything the family sent to care for her in Belgium.

Summary of Race and Class Representations in Letters from Rifka. The instances of race and class representations in the novel were saddening. The family had to flee Russia because of their Jewish ethnicity. For them, racism did not begin in America but rather was the push factor that brought them here.

The family was poor in Russia, and coming to America was not easy either. They had to work on the Sabbath, the Jewish day of rest, in order to support the family. However, their acclimation to American life was made easier because they already had children living in America.

Journey to America by Sonia Levitin (1970)

***Race Representations in* Journey to America.** Lisa, Ruth, Annie, and their parents, Mr. and Mrs. Platt, embarked on a dangerous journey as they emigrated from Germany in 1938 with hopes of coming to America. Mr. Platt came first so he could work and send for his children. While the Platts could afford to travel together, it would have been suspicious to see the entire family leaving Germany together. Mrs. Platt and the girls traveled to Zurich under the guise of a vacation and awaited their tickets to America there.

Jewish citizens were forbidden to see non-Jewish doctors because of their racial identification; thus, they depended on the Jewish doctors who could still practice. Lisa's best friend could not leave because her father, as the only doctor, felt he had to stay for his patients. He felt "his first duty was to the sick" (31).

The family faced racial prejudice as they traveled out of Germany on their way to Switzerland. They were forced to disembark and their luggage was searched to ensure that they were not taking any valuables with them. Lisa was angry that they were treated in this demeaning manner. As far as she could determine, they looked just like the other Russian natives, yet they were being discriminated against because they were Jews.

While they waited in Zurich for Mr. Platt to send for them, Mrs. Platt and the girls received terrible news about the fate of other Jewish people back home in Germany. Lisa found out that her aunt and uncle had been killed in the senseless massacre. They were dead not because they did or said anything but simply because of their race; because they were Jews!

***Class Representations in* Journey to America.** In America, Mr. Platt began a new phase of his life. He did not have a business as he had back in Germany, and he had to resort to jobs that he would normally not have done. When he wrote home, the children were shocked at this change for their father. This was not how they pictured life in America. Mrs. Platt admonished the girls not to tell their grandmother. Mr. Platt's mother thought he was being too hasty in leaving Germany. She would not be happy to learn that her son's socioeconomic status was so diminished. Mr. Platt was doing menial work and living in substandard conditions in order to save his family from the persecution they undoubtedly faced in Germany.

As Mrs. Platt prepared to leave on her "vacation," her maid implored her to take some of her prized possessions. Knowing the danger they faced, she refused. The family left their fine silver, paintings, jewels, and home behind to live in a place where their socioeconomic level would be lower.

The family suffered much hardship in Zurich. Mrs. Platt ran out of money and the children had to be sent to a foster care camp. There, thirteen-year-old Lisa slept in a crib because beds were scarce. Finally, they met some kind people who took the children in and helped Mrs. Platt until her husband could send for them. When the approval for them to travel finally came, the family was able to travel comfortably.

They were spared the harsh treatment that poor passengers who travel in steerage went through. The journey was "like one long vacation from day to day…" (146). Their trip was more in line with the lives they led before escaping to Zurich.

Summary of Race and Class Representations in Journey to America. The Platts suffered discrimination, which forced them to leave their comfortable lifestyle, family, and friends. Although their actions in leaving Germany seemed hasty, the massacre that happened shortly after they left proved Mr. Platt was correct in his decision to leave. Discrimination causes senseless acts of violence and affects victims in horrific ways. The Platts' experiences highlight how different people's lives can be in different situations.

Silver Days by Sonia Levitin (1989)

Race Representations in Silver Days. *Silver Days* continues the story after the Platts' ordeal of leaving Germany and coming to America. It chronicles the family's experiences in America as they tried to make their dreams of a better life and a more tolerable atmosphere for racial differences come true. Lisa soon discovered that there were racial tensions in America too. Her teacher called her "stupid" (9) because she did not know that "lavatory" meant a bathroom.

She had just arrived in America and was trying to adjust to a new system and to learn English, but her teacher seemed oblivious of these facts. A teacher who was expected to champion the causes of her students called Lisa stupid because she did not recognize an English word for bathroom.

Lisa soon realized that in America other people also discriminate against them because they are Jewish. As they rode their new friend Lester's bike, his father became angry and abusive: "And what in tarnation is that little kike doing with your bicycle?…I told you to stay away from them, didn't I?" (16). Although they seemed to be on the same socioeconomic level, Lester's father obviously thought the Platts were not good enough to play with his son because they were Jews.

Color is a major factor that worked in the family's favor. Mr. Platt told his family that if they became American citizens, they would be just like anybody else. Because of their skin color, becoming Americans could provide them with the dominant cultural capital others had and craved. They could be like mainstream Americans.

The stereotypical image of the black cleaning lady overshadowed Mrs. Platt's attempts to get ahead. As she went out trying to find a job to help her husband, she was discriminated against because everybody preferred black servants or maids. Black women were supposedly better domestic workers than white women.

The family's own position on race comes to the fore as Mr. Platt voiced disgust that black women were considered better domestic workers than his wife, and later, as the family encounters new neighbors. Lisa confides in her diary: "A terrible family moved in next door... Mother says they are Polish. She says the Polish are low-class" (109). This assumption is based on Mrs. Platt's encounter with one Polish family.

***Class Representations in* Silver Days.** When Lisa, her sisters, and her mother reached New York, everything looked so beautiful; she was sure her father had become rich. He was wearing a woolen suit and a hat and spoke in English to the bus driver. They were excited that Mr. Platt was "so American!" (2).

Mr. Platt's appearance portrayed an image of wealth. His suit was wool. He was speaking English. Everything must be great then. They would go back to living as they had been accustomed to in Germany. Instead, the dreary looking house he took them to belied that notion. Their socioeconomic class in America would definitely not be the elite lifestyle they had been accustomed to in Germany. The reality was unexpected.

The reality of their socioeconomic status became more obvious when Mrs. Platt brought home secondhand clothes from her job. Ruth and Lisa were very excited because the clothes were beautiful and were obviously expensive. Lisa wore one of the beautiful sweaters to school and was very dismayed when a young girl approached and said that Lisa was wearing her sweater. Unconcerned that she had just embarrassed Lisa about the sweater, the girl ran off to be with her friends.

Things started to improve for the family after Mr. Platt moved them to California. They found a nice house, and the parents gained stable jobs. Signs of financial improvement were evident when Mr. Platt made a beautiful coat sample that promised to be a big seller.

The family had finally arrived. Mr. Platt was doing what he loved to do best. The family moved into a "house, a real house separate from all others" (116), and soon Mr. Platt bought a car. For Lisa, her family's improved status was evident from the individualized name label her father had sewn to the sleeve of the sample coat.

Summary of Race and Class Representations in Silver Days. The premise of this book is that even though some people are discriminated against because of their race, if they are determined enough they can succeed in America. While the family seemed concerned with racial prejudice, it only surfaced when Mrs. Platt needed to find a job or when the girls played with their friend in New York. As their financial status improved, this prejudice seemed less important. The family's desperate measures to survive financially were overshadowed by the reality that things were not all that bad. After all, the children never had to work to help support the family, and when they did help their father as he opened his own business, all their earnings went into their savings accounts to spend as they wished. The implication of the Platt family's experiences, considering that they were immigrants, is that they were so industrious that they did well even after all they had to endure.

The Cat Who Escaped from Steerage by Evelyn W. Mayerson (1990)

Class Representations in The Cat Who Escaped from Steerage. This novel was very short and only related Chanah and her family's experiences journeying from Poland to America. The representations in this story were mainly based on class issues.

The family was so poor that they had only the clothes they were wearing, "five dollars in gold...linens, four down-filled pillows, a comforter, brass candlesticks, a pot to cook in, a wooden bucket...two silver cups...and ten English words" (2–3). They hid everything of value so no one would steal from them. They traveled in steerage because that was all they could afford.

Chanah, who had smuggled a stray cat aboard with her, got to explore the ship as she searched for her runaway cat. The visions she saw of the other sections and levels of the boat surprised her. There were "floor-to-ceiling mirrors, doorways with portieres of crimson velvet" (27) and other valuable treasures her family could only dream of. While her family struggled to get accustomed to their voyage in the dingy steerage compartment at the bottom of the ship, there were those "rich folks" above them who were enjoying luxurious lifestyles.

The class difference is obvious when Chanah and her cousin were caught on the upper deck and brought back below with stern warnings that they did not belong upstairs. After all, they were "children from steerage" (38). Passengers on the upper deck did not want to be seen talking to passengers from steerage. They did not want anything to affect their social standing when they landed in America. As long as they did not have to fraternize with the poor travelers, they could pretend that everything was going well.

The class difference is even more evident as the passengers prepared to disembark in New York. While the "poor" passengers from steerage struggled with their luggage, passengers from the upper deck threw money down to them as if they were beggars. The "rich" passengers enjoyed seeing the poor children fight to get the precious coins they threw at them. Chanah's father, Yonkel, cautioned his children not to pick up anything. He told them that in America they would be rich soon. Their life in America would be far better than having to scramble for coins.

Although he was poor, Yonkel was determined that his family's socioeconomic status in America would be better than it was in Poland. He was headed to New Jersey to live on a farm and was determined that nothing would change his mind. Although he was taking the family to a farm community, he was determined that his children would have an education in America, especially his daughter. Chanah was responsible for helping her cousin, who was mute, gain entrance into the United States.

Summary of Class Representations in **The Cat Who Escaped from Steerage.** Class representations indicate that poor people come to America with big dreams of being prosperous. Many have lofty goals of how they will fulfill these dreams. The poor people in this novel, although they had limited education, were determined that life for their children would be different. Their children would be educated. Education, then, would allow these children to lead better lives than their parents had. The book also suggests that even though these people were poor, they had the right attitude needed to become Americans. This attitude would allow them to assimilate with minimal difficulty since they were open to the changes life in the new world promised. They knew the standards in American would be different from the ones in their "old" country and they were willing to quickly adapt these new standards.

Land of Hope by Joan L. Nixon (1992)

***Race Representations in* Land of Hope.** Race representations stand out in this novel as groups of people from various countries congregated in steerage on their way to a better life in America. When Rebekah questioned why people who spoke English needed to emigrate to America, a new acquaintance explained that the immigrants were not English, they were "mostly Irish" (21). The Irish were not English. That distinction was clear.

As the passengers were forced to live together in close proximity, they often fought because their customs were different: "Now and again there were angry voices raised in argument as boundaries were overstepped or one person behaved as was customary in his culture, not knowing he was offending someone from another country" (33).

When the family landed and got settled in New York, one of Rebekah's brothers became involved in a gang. He learned early to fight to maintain his Jewish territory. Members of different racial groups stayed on their "end of the block." Whenever boundaries were crossed, they had to defend their honor.

The Irish girl who befriended Rebekah on the voyage to America settled in Boston and found work as a clerk. She was very excited about this job because she had been sure her only job prospect was to be "a maid for rich people" (156). The Irish maid stereotype comes out here. Rose has done well for herself because she did not have to come here and be a maid like other Irish girls had done.

***Class Representations in* Land of Hope.** Class differences were evident before Rebekah embarked on her immigrant journey. As she stood waiting to board the ship, she realized that there were different types of people aboard. Many were dressed in elegant clothes. Rebekah knew these clothes were expensive so she did not yearn for them. However, she envisioned her father, an accomplished tailor, making and selling such fine clothes in America.

As the family traveled to America, Rebekah's grandfather, who had been a scholar in Russia, explained that different classes of people were treated differently when they reached America. First- and second-class passengers did not go through the rigorous examination at Ellis Island because they could continue to support themselves. This example highlights that if you had money, America welcomed you with opened arms. If you didn't, you had to pass the litmus test in order to be accepted.

Rebekah's family realized how demanding life in America could be. They had to work from dark to dark every day just to make enough money to pay their living expenses. Deeply religious, the family found that they could not keep the Sabbath as they wanted. Rebekah's hope of one day going to college and becoming an educated young woman began to seem more remote. Her hope for the future was renewed when she met a female teacher at the HIAS (Hebrew Immigrant Aid Society) center. The teacher explained that her family had had the same early struggles but they worked hard and were able to move out of the slum. She wished the same for Rebekah. Mrs. Meyer's message of hope to Rebekah was that "this too will pass." Rebekah realized for the first time that not everyone in America went through the same lowly conditions her family experienced. Mrs. Meyer's talk gave her hope that things could indeed be different if she worked hard enough.

Summary of Race and Class Representations in Land of Hope. *Land of Hope* suggests that immigrants of different racial groups, settled into the same types of jobs as the immigrants who came before them. Like his brother, Rebekah's father resigns himself to the drudgery of the sweatshop. Already an established coat designer, he gives up all dreams of making fine coats and going into business for himself. Although the family works very hard, there does not seem to be room for improved socioeconomic standards. They just seem to be existing from day to day, hoping to make enough money to pay their living expenses.

Another issue that comes out very explicitly is one that has not really been a focus of this study: the issue of gender. Rebekah was smarter than her brothers. Her grandfather taught her several languages and she was good at keeping the family thinking ahead about their future. Although Rebekah yearned to go to school, her mother felt this was a waste, as

Rebekah was expected to get married and have children. When her parents saw how determined she was to further her education, they reluctantly relented. They did not understand why, but the resounding theme that "this was America and anything could happen" came through. Her determination, however, helped Rebekah's father to see that perhaps he too could fulfill his dreams of making designer coats in the new country. America was a land where ultimately, dreams could be fulfilled.

Good-bye to the Trees by Vicky Shiefman (1993)

***Race Representations in* Good-bye to the Trees.** This book is another example of how racial and economic oppression force one group of people to seek refuge in another country. Thirteen-year-old Fagel came from a large family and her father was dead. While the family suffered in Russia, Fagel's mother sought ways to send her children to places where they could learn trades and help themselves. Fagel, trained to be a dressmaker, was sent to Boston. On the journey, Fagel met one young woman who had suffered a hideous ordeal. Her house had been burned and she had just managed to escape with her baby. The young woman had suffered not because of anything she had said or done, but because she was Jewish.

Fagel quickly found out that people of different backgrounds kept to themselves in Boston. Every racial group had its clearly defined boundaries, and it was obvious that these boundaries were respected and no one crossed them.

***Class Representations in* Good-bye to the Trees.** As Fagel entered her aunt and uncle's home in Boston, she realized that there were a lot of people living there. She worried that her aunt would not be able to take care of her. Later, as her aunt confided in her, Fagel realized that the family was indeed experiencing economic hardships. Her uncle was sickly and kept a job only because he was working in a family business. Her aunt worried about how she and her children would survive if anything should happen to him.

Afraid to go to school because she didn't want to look like a "green horn," Fagel stayed home with her aunt and sewed. One day Mrs. Goodman, the woman she sewed for, asked her to be a maid. Fagel was furious that her training as a dressmaker was being ignored and that she was asked to be a maid. She determined that "rich people think they're better than poor people and that they can buy us" (51). She had worked very hard to become a dressmaker. She was angry that people with money treated those without as if they were nothing. They always assumed that poor people wanted to be maids or work in other apparently "demeaning" jobs.

Determined to help her family, Fagel decided to take the job with Mrs. Goodman. She would still be a dressmaker but would work to obtain the money she needed to help her brothers and sisters join her in America. Fagel found Mrs. Goodman interesting. Mrs. Goodman wanted to be "American" in every sense of the word. She wanted to have a nanny for her children. She also wanted her children to be "American" thus she named them after famous people in the society pages. Mrs. Goodman felt that if she patterned her life after the "Americans," then surely she would be American too.

***Summary of Race and Class Representations in* Good-bye to the Trees.** The premise of race in this story showed that people of different races stayed with their own kind. Fagel came to America but her life was completely centered on people who shared the same customs and language. Class representations are more obvious. Poor people worried about how their families would be taken care of, but they did not plan for the future. Fagel's aunt was expecting her seventh child, even though the family was already experiencing economic strains. As people gained higher socioeconomic status, they displayed actions that clearly define American values.

Good-bye Billy Radish by Gloria Skurzynski (1992)

***Race Representations in* Good-bye Billy Radish.** In this novel the genuine friendship between two boys, an American and an immigrant, that lasts many years is heartwarming. This is the second case in the novels being studied that such a strong bond was identified. Young Hank was American because he was born here and his father had also been born in America. They were clearly Americans. Although the Americans talked to the immigrants, racial boundaries were still evident in where people lived. This division did not deter Hank and Billy from developing a strong relationship.

The Americans were intrigued that the most influential man in town, the general superintendent of the mills, was married to an Ukrainian immigrant. Although the superintendent's house was the most marvelous creation in the town, his wife became the main attraction when the villagers attended Hank's sister's wedding there.

Racial difference is illuminated in the way different groups observed each other. They did not like each other, but they could tolerate each other's presence in the name of religion. Billy's father hated the Russians, but the family attended a Russian church since there is no Ukrainian Orthodox church in America. Billy explained to Hank, "It's complicated. Ukrainians hate Russia, but they don't hate the church. The church is God. Nobody can hate God" (75). Although they hated each other, different racial groups who worshipped the same God put aside their hatred in order to worship. This seems strange since the premise of religion is one based on loving your brother as yourself.

When Billy celebrated his "passage into manhood" on his fourteenth birthday, Hank joined him. Billy's father offered a toast to Hank honoring the friendship the two boys had shared over the years. Billy's father insisted that "in America, people from different villages can be like brothers" (77). However, this seems more true for children than for adults. As the Ukrainian family demonstrated their appreciation of the boys' friendship, Hank swelled with pride. He was a "real American, the only one in the room born in America" (77). Hank's revered status as a native-born American citizen made him the honored person in a large group of immigrants. Even though many of the Ukrainians had gained citizenship through immigration naturalization processes, they were still not "truly American."

Class Representations in **Good-bye Billy Radish.** Difference in class status is evident in the way people were treated according to the level of jobs they had. No one overstepped his or her boundaries. Mr. Bonner, the general superintendent of the steel mills where the majority of the citizens are employed, was held in highest esteem.

When he tried to be jovial at the wedding celebration, no one was sure how to react. Mr. Bonner was "as powerful as God" (60) and everyone was afraid of offending him. Thus, even though they were at a social function, the atmosphere remained very tense. Even Hank and Billy (who was invited because he was Hank's friend) were warned not to do anything to offend Mr. Bonner or bring shame on Hank's parents.

Although Billy had grown up in America, his position as a working immigrant child is evident in his leaving school at the age of fourteen to assume a full-time position in the mill. Billy and his family were now American citizens, but in this community, the only upward mobility for the immigrants came from working in the steel mills. Thus, Billy began his twelve-hour shifts working alongside the men in the mills.

Hank hated the idea that one day he too would have to join his father in the steel mill. Although his father was a foreman and Hank's position would be above the immigrants, he was unhappy about the prospects of doing this work the rest of his life. A stroke of fate helped Hank to decide what he wanted to be when he grew up. He helped his sister-in-law to deliver her baby during a terrible snowstorm and decided his future career then.

He visited Billy, who was very sick with influenza, to share the good news. "I decided what I'm gonna be…A doctor. I don't care how long it takes. I'll even work in the mill if I have to, to get enough money to go to medical college" (124). Hank wanted a better life than the steel mill had to offer. Although he hated the thought of working in the mill, he would work there to support himself through college. If he were a doctor, he could prescribe medication to make his best friend well.

When Billy died, Hank was heartbroken. He became more resolute in his decision to become a doctor. He was determined to stop people from dying. He couldn't save lives if he became a steel mill worker. His ambitions surpassed following in his father's footsteps to be a supervisor in the mills. Being "American" gave Hank the privilege to think outside the accepted norms of his community and family. His ambitions also clearly defined him as an American. His dreams of becoming a doctor emphasizes the "children will do better than their parents did" motto.

***Summary of Race and Class Representations in* Good-bye Billy Radish.** In this novel race issues indicate that even if you become a naturalized American citizen, you were still an immigrant. One positive aspect of this book, however, was the strong bond between Billy and Hank. Their friendship epitomizes the innocence of childhood. While adults dutifully maintained their distance from each other, openly acknowledging and honoring their racial differences, children were unconcerned with such matters. They saw each other as friends, not as immigrants and Americans.

Class issues were evident not only in the fact that the American workers had better jobs than the immigrants but also in the level of comradeship between the American families themselves. The higher the position they held in the mill, the less interaction they had with others of lower socioeconomic levels.

The Star Fisher by Laurence Yep (1991)

Race Representations in The Star Fisher. As the Lee family disembarked from the train, they had dreams of starting a new life in Virginia. They would open a bigger laundry establishment and their hopes of saving enough money for the future seemed promising. However, as they prepared to leave the train station, they encountered their first brush with racism as the town nuisance called them "darn monkeys" (7).

Without knowing the family, this individual (an American) started name-calling. His hatred was based solely on the fact that the Lees were of Chinese origin. He was not accustomed to seeing them in his neighborhood. They did not fit in. They were different. Eight-year-old Emily rebelled against this name-calling by purposely stepping on the offender's foot. He quickly forgot his anger as he tried to fathom the incredible fact that the children spoke English:

> "She talks American." "Of course we do," Emily snapped. "We were born here. We go to American schools." Mister Snuff's [Joan's name for the stranger because he was chewing snuff] jaw dropped open. "They both talk." (8)

He could not believe that Chinese people could speak English. Even though they were living in America, this fact proved highly incredible.

Joan became upset at her mother, as more and more her mother depended on her to face the outside community. As her mother's dependency became more obvious, Joan critically viewed her helplessness. "I saw her with American eyes: saw the little woman with the funny skin and the odd eyes" (72). In her eyes, her mother fit the stereotype that others held of Chinese physical features.

Joan experienced overt signs of racism as Miss Lucy, their landlord, took the family to visit a local church for the first time. A woman with "silver-blue" hair snubbed her nose when she saw them entering. Quite noticeably, while the adults expressed racist attitudes toward them, the younger children did not. Emily and Bobby, ages eight and ten respectively, were welcomed by the children in their age groups and blended in with no problem. The girls in Joan's age group (sixteen years old) ignored her and even snickered as she went by.

Mrs. Lee made a pie to be auctioned off at the church's bake sale. However, the family was unprepared for the reaction from the church-people. No one would bid. In order to save face, the Reverend ended up buying the pie for twenty-five cents when the other pies went for at least two dollars.

Mr. Snuff continued to haunt the Lees by spraying hate words on their fence and standing by grinning as Mr. Lee came out and tried to wash away the hateful words. When Miss Lucy, who had been his elementary school teacher, threatened to have him arrested, he was unfazed. He called her a "chink lover" and exclaimed that her charges against him would "never stick" (138). As far as he was concerned, Miss Lucy's case against him would be futile because the Lees were Chinese. He felt assured that nothing would happen to him in a court of law. After all, the Lees were not Americans, but he was.

***Class Representations in* The Star Fisher.** Joan became very concerned with her parents' financial status after they settled in. Although her parents had opened for business, they had no customers. Mrs. Lee tried to keep the finances in order by spending as sparingly as she could. When the town's grocer offered to extend credit to the Lees, Joan knew her father would not accept it. He was too proud. He worked hard for a living and did not want handouts. Her father was a learned man who would have had a high position in China if the Communist government had not taken over. Now, in America, he had to struggle to make a living.

As an outsider, Joan had difficulty making friends. Her first attempt to be friendly was contemptuously ignored. She finally made friends with Bernice, another outsider. Bernice was white, like the other students, but she was treated as an outsider because her family were "theater people." Joan understood. Theater people were "not very respectable either in China or in America" (89). Although Bernice's family was probably at the same financial level as many of the other families, their occupation as traveling theater entertainers diminished their socioeconomic status and respectability with the others.

ed to shape the later
perienced fluctuating
promise in his or her
before she was able to
seemed she would not
o gain acceptance, and
n her way home, the
s to be anything she
for her.

backs when they first
ned to, her father was
ily quickly overcame
in California and Mr.
ts and bought a car.
d Lisa felt happy that
."

l destination, but her
would be all right for
ation for his children,
New York where the
Her high intellectual

rk sweatshop, where
moaned the way her
America. Her father
fine clothes he was
o working under his
to fulfill her dreams
ht school.

naid. She dreamed of
r family. When her
fronted her and then
to pay for a sibling's
o bring the rest of the

pants before he was
He enjoyed life as a
town fair. However,
job at the steel mill.

As Joan witnessed Bernice's negative reactions to her own family's situation, she realized that although she was treated differently because of her race she did not want to let other people cause her to disrespect or hate her family. Bernice was so adamant about being different from her family, about speaking properly, and about being called by her formal name. She felt that these attributes would ensure her improved status with the mainstream Americans. She wanted to fit in with them.

Joan realized that an esteemed class status was also very important for her parents. Her parents' dream was to work hard and save enough money to return to live in China in their later years. Mrs. Lee told Joan, "When we have enough money, we'll live in China at a level appropriate to your father's status" (100). In America, the family had no appreciated status among the Americans, but in China things would be different. Mrs. Lee could have servants and Mr. Lee's educational expertise would be respected. This was a priceless hope for Mr. and Mrs. Lee.

Summary of Race and Class Representations in The Star Fisher. The presence of racism in this novel demonstrates how people allow preconceived notions to form negative opinions about other people who are different from them. Even though the "upstanding members" of the community did not call the Lees derogatory names or spray paint their fences with hate words, they maintained their distance from the Lees. Many did not begin to patronize the Lees' laundry until Miss Lucy called them and asked them to show a united front that they did not share the same views as "Mr. Snuff." The others in the community were just as guilty as Mr. Snuff. They were simply more subtle in their attitude.

Mrs. Lee's character did not endear her to anyone initially. Her distrust for everyone, even her landlord, Miss Lucy, who offered to teach her to cook, made her appear to be an ungrateful immigrant who did not know how to appreciate the goodness of others.

While the villagers did not openly express their racist attitude toward the Lees, they were not as subtle about Bernice and her family, who were like them but whom they held in lower esteem. Not only did they express their disapproval of Bernice's family, they wanted nothing to do with Bernice. Regardless of how hard she tried to fit in, Bernice remained an outcast. Differences in class positions illuminated the town's intolerance with their "own." While they eventually allowed the Lees, a Chinese family, to be accepted into the daily milieu of the town's life, Bernice's family, a white family, did not get this opportunity.

Combined Analysis of the
in the Middle Immigration Wav

Different racial and class representations
analysis of the eight middle wave immigrant
relate tales of Jewish immigrant experiences.
about the same time period, the varied e
characters emphasized that there were differ
lation of the various racial groups.

Who Are the Immigrants?

The stories are distinct in the way the in
portrayed. All but one of the protagonists ar
from Rifka, Lisa in *Journey to America* and
Cat Who Escaped from Steerage, Rebekah
Good-bye to the Trees, and Joan in *The Sta*
onist is Billy, the young boy in *Good-bye B*
only character who was born in Americ;
experience of traveling to America.

Where Do They Come From?

The novels represent people from different
journeys with her family from Russia; Lisa
Germany; Chanah's family comes from Pol;
journey from Russia; Fagel travels alone fro
ily emigrated from the Ukraine; and Joan is
Ohio to immigrant parents.

What Are Their Experiences Before and ,

Before Experiences. The characters in th
shared some similarities but there were
beginning experiences. Rifka in *Letters fro*
in Russia. The Jewish family could not hav
item in their home because they wer

After Experiences. Different circumstances serv
experiences of the seven protagonists. Most e;
circumstances, but for the most part each shows
after experiences. Rifka suffered several setbacks
enter the United States. Finally, on arrival, it still
be accepted. Her superior intelligence helped her t
although at the end of the story she was just c
immigration official's confidence in her abilitie
wanted to be gave hope that life would be all right

Although Lisa and her family suffered some se
arrived (the house wasn't what they were accustor
a peddler, her mother had to be a maid), the fan
these. Soon they were able to rent a nice house
Platt resumed his own business making fine co;
Ruth, the oldest daughter, prepared for college, ar
the family's successes meant that they had "arrived

Chanah's family had not yet reached their fin;
father's focused determination suggests that things
them. He had the right mindset. He wanted an edu
especially his daughters. He would not stay in
entire family had to work just to make ends meet
abilities proved that she should go to school.

Rebekah learned the drudgery of the New Y(
everybody worked to support the family. She be
parents gave up their dreams of a better life in
didn't even have the courage to start making the
capable of making but instead resigned himself
brother's demanding schedule. Rebekah determine
of one day going to college and started to attend ni;

Fagel put her sewing skills on hold to become a
saving enough money to send for the rest of h
employer stole her money, Fagel determinedly co
walked away from the job. She sent home money
passage to America, and determined to work hard t
family to America.

Billy was the only boy in his town to wear lon;
fourteen. This made him the envy of the other boys
boy, playing with his friend Hank and going to the
at fourteen he quit school and assumed a full-time

Shortly after his transition into manhood, he contracted influenza in the mill and died before reaching his fifteenth birthday.

After some setbacks, the Lees' family business was up and running. While they had had to eat "lettuce" sandwiches for fear of running out of money when they first arrived, the family could once again afford to eat regular meals. Mrs. Lee also learned to cook so the family had fewer burnt meals. Joan made friends and did not feel so lonely anymore. Although she helped her parents in the laundry after school, she was also able to visit with friends and have private time.

How Are Issues of Race and Class Represented in the Novels?

The critique of the race and class representations conducted in the first section of the analysis of the middle immigration wave novels speaks specifically to the main and subquestions for question 2.

How Are Characters Racially Identified?

Six of the protagonists in the middle immigration novels were white, while the seventh protagonist was Asian. All the characters at some point were considered to be outsiders by the mainstream American society. All, like the immigrants of the early immigration wave, were distinguished by their country of origin, and in the case of the Jews, by their Jewish ethnicity.

Are Issues of Race and Class Present in the Novels?

The individual issues of race and class have been discussed at length at the beginning of the analytic process. Instances of race and class representations of immigrants were identified in varying degrees in the eight novels. Each book addressed different aspects of race and class according to the context of each story. In *Letters from Rifka*, racial representation of the immigrants was in the form of oppression and persecution because they were Jews. Rifka's experiences in America had not been marred because she had still not arrived in America. She experienced class differences in the way she saw different immigrants being treated before they were released into America and in her parents' experiences of working on the Sabbath to support the family.

In *Journey to America* and *Silver Days*, Lisa experienced racial prejudice when her teacher called her stupid because she didn't know what a "lavatory" was and when the neighbor refused to let his son play with her and her sister. She questioned her Jewish ethnicity, wondering if life would have been different for them if they were not Jews. Her mother was refused employment because she was not black. The employer felt that a black maid would do a better job than Mrs. Platt could. Class status for them started on a downward spin before things got better. Coming from a refined home in Germany where they had a maid, the Platts had to live in substandard housing before they were able to improve their socioeconomic status.

Chanah had minimal contacts with other passengers from other countries; she stayed mainly with her family members. They were poor immigrants, but the father exhibited a cultured outlook on life that suggests that the family would make it in America. He had the "know-how" to succeed. After all, hard work was all that was needed to become rich and American.

In *Land of Hope* racism is the push factor that sent Rebekah and her family to America. She witnessed how the poison of racism can cause tremendous damage as her brother joins a gang and fights to protect the Jewish territory in a racially divided city. While the family came with high hopes of making a good living, the low socioeconomic level they found themselves in contributed to her parents' resigned acceptance of their fate. Rebekah learned that people are able to rise above such terrible beginnings and make their own life decisions. She was determined to go to college so she could improve her socioeconomic status.

In *Good-bye to the Trees*, Fagel learned that racism causes people extreme hardships, breaks families apart, and totally destroys people's lives. She learned that in America, people of the same racial background stick together, and she learned to identify the different racially segregated communities. Fagel also learned that as people move up the socioeconomic ladder they care less for people below them.

In *Good-bye Billy Radish*, Billy became friends with an American boy who taught him to speak English. They enjoyed life as children, doing things they both liked. While Billy experienced racism outside of his relationship with Hank, this story portrays his acclimation to American mainstream life as a positive experience. Although Billy started working at the age of fourteen, he was still able to save some of his money for his personal expenses. Life was not so terrible for the family that they had to struggle to survive. The family owned their own home and made time for huge family parties and fun time.

Finally, in *The Star Fisher*, Joan experienced overt racism from a street bum but realized that the mainstream townspeople were not much different in their feelings. They were just not as blatant as "Mr. Snuff" was. She understood that people discriminated against her family not because of what they did or said but simply because of their Chinese features.

Do These Images Change for Different Immigrant Groups?

The images presented of the different immigrant groups differ quite markedly for different protagonists. Their acclimation to the American mainstream life was different. Those who came with family members faired better than those who came without. Somehow, their acclimation to the new world seemed aided by the fact that they had others around them who were also learning "new rules" and adjusting to "new" life in general.

How Are Different Immigrant Groups Presented?

The various immigrant groups in the novels are represented differently. Rifka was an innocent, caring girl who could not resist doing something good for others. This eventually became her saving grace, as the immigration doctor praised her unselfishness to the immigration officials.

Fagel and Rebekah are the only two girls who had to work full-time jobs to help their families. While Joan also worked, her job was treated as simply helping out her parents after school. Billy became a man as he went out to work one day after his fourteenth birthday. Lisa's life was the most sheltered. She did not have to work to supplement her family's income.

Although many of the families experienced hardships, the stories portray a sense that life was not too difficult after all. Everyone was able to get jobs, even if the jobs were not what they wanted. Except for Fagel and Billy, the children did not have to go out on the streets to find jobs. They worked in the confines of their homes.

How Do Characters Handle Cross-Cultural Encounters?

The characters share some similarities in the way they handled cross-cultural interactions. They all received some level of education and except for Billy, who left school at fourteen, each of the remaining characters determined to further her education by taking advantage of the educational system that America offers. All of the characters eagerly embraced facets of the American culture. Chanah's father knows that his daughter is smart. He also knows that in America, although she is a girl, she can get a good education. Lisa and her sisters quickly embraced the opportunities that American schools offered. Fagel stayed home and learned English because she did not want to be a "greenhorn." Finally she went to school with dreams of getting an education and helping to bring the rest of her family to America. Rebekah held on to her dreams of going to college even after her family insisted that she should get married and stay at home. Seeing her determination, however, her parents grudgingly agreed for her to go to school. Only in America could she achieve such lofty ambitions of becoming educated. Each character endorsed the American culture with strong faith and belief that things would work for the better.

Historical Evaluation of Middle Immigration Novels

Although the novels had episodes where the issues of race and class presented a negative representation of immigrants in the middle immigration wave, generally their acclimation seemed positive. The history of the middle immigration wave highlights mixed treatment of the immigrants. True to the history of when they came, the characters came either before or after the 1921 immigration act, which restricted the inflow of immigrants from the countries the middle wave immigrants came from: eastern Europe and China.

The experiences of the Jewish immigrants were related to the tales from Russia and Germany. The history surrounding the Jews portrays images of them fleeing their native countries simply because of their religious backgrounds, leaving everything of value behind. When they arrive in America, they suffer at first but soon are able to excel because of their determination. The Platts' family was exemplary.

The negative treatment of the Lees (although their experiences seem fairly mild compared to the atrocities suffered by many Chinese immigrants) is consistent with the way Chinese immigrants of the period were treated. The story even addresses the Chinese-American stereotypical image of owning a Laundromat.

The Ukrainians' love of the church is evidenced by Billy's family attending a Russian church because they did not have an orthodox Ukrainian church in the city. They did this even though they disliked the Russians.

Although this study did not focus on the gender issue, this topic was evident in several of the novels. For example, in *Land of Hope*, Rebekah was smarter than her two brothers. She spoke several languages and her communication skills were great. When she asked to go to school, her parents refused. They felt that an education for Rebekah would be wasted, since she was expected to marry and have children. Rebekah had the courage to tell her parents (something she would not have done at home) that she would go to college. Seeing her determination, they agreed. Chanah, Rifka, Lisa, and Joan also showed strong promise of doing well in school.

The realities of how young immigrants' lives were affected were further illuminated when Billy contracted influenza while working in the steel mill and died. His dreams of what he would do as an adult were shattered, as he died before his fifteenth birthday. Overall, life in the middle immigration period seems far removed from that of the early immigration wave. For the main characters in the novels, the experiences of living in America offered bright prospects for the future. They would be able to go to school, become better educated than their parents were, and be able to lead more fulfilling lives.

The experiences of the immigrants in the middle immigration wave allude to the fact that the Americans were not the problem in the race and class issues that were identified in the novels. Each immigrant came to America for a specific reason. For many, the push factor for them leaving their countries in the first place was that they were experiencing negative treatment from their own countrymen. Thus, the immigrants brought these problems with them; they were not here to begin with. America is not bad because it became the "saving grace" country that took them in when their own countries did not offer them solace. America took in strangers (immigrants, refugees, displaced persons, and other labeled groups), and in a very short time span these individuals have succeeded. They own their own businesses, and only people who exhibit "un-American" traits pose problems for them. For example, the Lees in *The Star Fisher* owned their laundry business, and the townspeople, with very little prodding from one of their own, became regular customers. The family's only brush with racism came from a street "bum," who was quickly put in his place by the townspeople.

Chapter 5

The New Immigration Wave: 1965–Present

The "third great wave" or new immigration wave period, which began in the late 1960s, continues today. This immigration period is strongly shaped by the Immigration and Naturalization Act of 1965, a series of refugee acts passed between 1961 and 1984, and by economic and political forces (Kellogg 1988). It differs from the early and middle immigration periods because the immigrants in the new immigration wave fall into three categories: legal immigrants, refugees, and undocumented immigrants. Legal immigrants are people who gain legal entry to the United States by utilizing the visa quota system. Refugees are people who flee their countries because of poverty, war, or violence. Undocumented, or illegal, immigrants encompass those who come through various channels but have not obtained resident visas. This wave of immigrants is among the largest in the history of the United States.

The Immigration Act of 1965 created major changes in the immigration policies that had been in effect since the late 1800s. This act abandoned the national origins quota system that gave priority to northern Europeans but limited entry of people from eastern and southern Europe (Keely 1986; Rolph 1992). People of Asian and black ancestry were the ones most negatively affected by the earlier quota system (Keely 1986). Although there were Asians in the earlier migratory periods, their numbers were in great disproportion to the European immigrants. While all Europeans were eligible for citizenship once they passed through Ellis Island, Asians had been denied this right (Christensen 1996). Blacks were involuntarily brought here as slaves; they had no constitutional rights, as they were regarded as only part human, definitely not equal to the ranks of the European immigrants. The 1965 laws changed many of these marginalized categorizations.

The Immigration Act of 1965 reversed several principles underlying earlier immigration legislation and shifted its focus to the humanitarian goal of supporting family unity. It capped immigration from the Western and Eastern Hemispheres but abandoned the strong preferential treatment accorded European countries by substituting uniform quotas of 20,000 visas per country for all countries. The act also allowed immediate family members of citizens and resident aliens to enter without numerical restrictions and outside of the quota.

The new act resulted in a decline in European immigration but a dramatic increase in Asian and Latin American immigration. Between 1961 and 1980, two out of every three immigrants came from Asia or Latin America (Rolph 1992). The 1965 act was a move to eliminate racial and ethnic discrimination in immigration, but it had new standards for excluding the "undesirable" immigrants. Immigrants now needed work certification, and the laws gave preference to middle and upper classes (Bandon 1994).

Since the 1965 Immigration Act, other immigration laws have been enacted to accommodate the needs of the various categories of immigrants. Congress enacted the Refugee Act of 1980 to monitor the process for admitting qualified refugees and to control the numbers and types of refugees being admitted yearly (Rolph 1992). This law set an annual limit for refugee immigration of 50,000.

Congress passed the 1986 Immigration Reform and Control Act in order to stem the tide of undocumented immigration. This law granted amnesty to long-term undocumented residents and special agricultural workers who had entered the country illegally. It also made it illegal to hire immigrants without proof of their citizenship or possession of a work visa (Bandon 1994; Rolph 1992).

The Immigration Act of 1990 addressed concerns that the existing regulations were not sufficiently responsive to the nation's economic requirements and that they discriminated against immigration from certain countries. It also established safeguards against illegal immigration by setting separate quotas for relatives of amnesty recipients, with the hope that reuniting undocumented aliens and their families would enhance the fight against illegal immigration (Bandon 1994; Rolph 1992). All these laws, passed over the years, have controlled in some sense how the "new immigrants" acclimate to the United States.

Who Are They?: People in the New Immigration Wave

This immigration wave consists mainly of members of various minority groups: Asians, Latin Americans, and West Indians. Although the "new" immigrants fall into various socioeconomic categories, not much is said about those who are quickly able to assimilate and contribute on a high level in American society. The portrayal of immigrants is usually of people coming to the United States to be charges of the governmental welfare system (Topolnicki 1995). Topolnicki further found that the vast majority of new immigrants, both legal and illegal, work very hard to help their families live better lives. Keely (1986) asserts that many of the opinions of today's immigrants are "impressionistic and anecdotal... [immigrants] are surely neither all good nor all bad" (179). He further asserts that studies conducted about immigrants are often done in an atmosphere of controversy and interpretations are based on preconceived notions.

Many of the new legal immigrant families coming to the United States are highly skilled, with Asian immigrants standing out among them (Keely 1986). However, many find that they have to work in lower-status jobs when they first immigrate in order to survive economically. For many new wave immigrants, education for their children is of top priority. The school system offers many resources and possibilities that were not available in their various homelands (Bandon 1994; First 1988; Keely 1986). The question of cultural assimilation or acculturation frequently arises around the issue of whether immigrants will acclimate to the American way of life. Will they become Americanized or will they hold on to their traditional way of life? Many factors influence the way the new wave immigrants are incorporated into American life.

The Salvadorans in the New Immigration Wave

Although the Salvadorans form the fourth largest group in the Latino population of the United States, very little is written about them, presumably because their arrival is more recent than that of other Latino groups (Mahler 1995). The Salvadoran population was small until the outbreak of civil warfare in El Salvador in 1979. During the decade following this outbreak, hundreds of thousands of Salvadorans fled their homeland, with the majority seeking refuge in the United States. Mahler describes that an estimated 70,000 people died before the war ended in 1992 when the warring parties signed peace treaties.

Most of the Salvadorans who sought refuge in the United States have been undocumented immigrants. Many were too afraid of retaliation in their country to apply for a visiting visa. They knew that they would be denied access because they were poor and they did not have family members who were already living in the United States. Mahler (1995) found that the "combination of poverty and fear discouraged almost everyone from contemplating applying" (9). She illustrates one immigrant's experience:

> If you go to the U.S. embassy to get a visa...you have to have a good job, a bank account, and the title of a house...then they will give you a visa so you can travel as a tourist. But if you don't have this, they won't give it to you...Two to three hundred persons go to the U.S. embassy every day and they may give a visa to 20 or 10. (9)

Since most of the people lived in poverty, they did not qualify for these visas.

In her study of Salvadoran immigrants in Long Island, New York, Mahler (1995) found that many of the immigrants are illiterate. Many earn low wages from which they have to support themselves and also send money home to El Salvador to support family members left behind. Because of their lack of fluency in the English language, they experience great difficulties in improving their socioeconomic status. A large number of Salvadoran immigrants obtained legal status when the 1986 Immigration Reform and Control Act made provisions for the legalization of certain categories of undocumented immigrants. Those who entered the United States before 1982 and others who had worked in agriculture were able to obtain legal permanent status. They in turn petitioned for their other family members to join them.

In recent years, however, many Salvadoran immigrants have been unable to obtain permanent legal status to live and work in the United States. Thus, the government regards them as illegal immigrants. Although the future in America does not look promising for them, Mahler (1995) finds that many Salvadorans, dissatisfied with the limited educational and job opportunities in their homeland, keep coming in search of a better future. Many will continue the cycle of working menial jobs to support themselves and their families, but others have and will continue to excel in the United States. Like many immigrant groups before them, the Salvadorans come in search of a better life. The knowledge that they may never share the same status as other heralded immigrant groups is not enough to stop them from trying to make a better life for their families.

The Japanese Americans in the New Immigration Wave

The major immigration period for the Japanese was in the late 1800s, after the Chinese Exclusion Act of 1882 restricted Chinese immigrants from entering the United States (O'Brien and Fugita 1991). Since there was still a need for farm laborers in the West, the Japanese immigrants were used to fill the labor void (Banks 1997), so their immigration was encouraged. Many immigrants came because of economic hardship in their homeland. They came with high hopes of making their fortunes and returning home. Like the Chinese, however, many stayed on and raised their families, becoming Japanese Americans. When the Japanese started to prosper, anti-Asian sentiment toward the "yellow peril" fueled by white settlers, extended beyond the Chinese to encompass Japanese immigrants (Banks 1997; Zinn 1995).

Anti-Japanese sentiment increased drastically after Japan bombed Pearl Harbor on December 7, 1941. Many Japanese Americans living on the West Coast and other areas were placed in concentration camps after President Roosevelt issued Executive Order No. 9066. This order wrongfully presumed that the Japanese Americans posed a threat to the welfare of the United States. While many fought in the war, the negative stereotype fueled by white nativists prevented them from obtaining the status they deserved.

The immigration wave from 1965 to the present has resulted in a more positive portrayal of Japanese Americans today. Japanese Americans are the smallest Asian immigrant population in America, due in part to the highly developed economy in their homeland. Despite their small numbers, the Japanese Americans are regarded as the "so-called model American ethnic minority because of their success in education, social class mobility, and low levels of crime, mental illness, and other social deviances" (Banks 1997: 456). They are highly represented in managerial, professional, and technical occupations and they have been very successful in "achieving a solid middle class standing in American society" (O'Brien and Fugita 1991: 1).

In 1988, Congress passed the American Civil Liberties bill which was signed into law by then-President Reagan. The bill provided an apology to the Japanese Americans for their wrongful internment during World War II and a $20,000 payment for each survivor of the internment. This bill helped to close a painful chapter on the Japanese Americans' past experiences in America.

The Mexicans in the New Immigration Wave

Mexican Americans have always been a part of the United States. Before the first Pilgrims landed at Plymouth Rock, Mexicans were living in Texas, which at the time was called the "Rio Grande Valley," and in the part of Mexico that became U.S. territory after the Mexican-American War (Bandon 1993). Thus, the first Mexican Americans were not really immigrants at all (De Garza 1973). As the Mexicans lost more land to white settlers, racial hostility and prejudice toward them began, and it increased with the creation of the new states of the Southwest. This negative attitude toward Mexican Americans still continues in the current immigration wave, although it may take varied forms.

The Mexican-American cultural influence has been very visible in American society, from foods to Spanish-named cities to architectural designs (Bandon 1993). Mexican Americans in the new immigration wave excel in every field from politics to sports (De Garza 1973), although there is a large population of undocumented immigrants or migrant farm workers. As the economy in Mexico causes people to emigrate in search of jobs to support their families, the undocumented group of immigrants has increased, particularly in California and Texas. However, technological advances have negatively impacted the Mexican work force and many find their living conditions are not much improved over those in Mexico. Strong nativist reactions to the increase in Asian and Latin American immigrants have fueled the continued prejudice against Mexicans in America.

Various laws have been passed in the new immigration wave to stem the rapid increase of immigrants crossing the Mexican border. Congress enacted the Immigration Reform and Control Act of 1986 in part to limit the rapid flow of undocumented immigrants. The English-only movement escalated in the 1980s in an effort to have English declared the official language in major cities where there is a strong Hispanic population. Some schools have eliminated their bilingual education program insisting there is no longer a need for it. California continues to be an influential center of nativist activities. The year 1994 marked the passage of Proposition 187, a law pro-posed to deny undocumented workers and their children schooling and nonemergency medical care. The enforcement of this law was later prohibited in a 1997 court decision. Despite the many setbacks for Mexican Americans in the United States, their population continues to increase rapidly.

The Southeast Asians in the New Immigration Wave

The Southeastern Asians who have settled in the United States in the new immigration wave consist of immigrants from Vietnam, Kampuchea (hereafter referred to as Cambodia), and Laos (Banks 1997). The majority of these immigrants came as refugees who fled their homelands in the aftermath of the Vietnamese war. They left their homes when the Communist government came to power at the end of the war. The Southeast Asian immigration prompted the largest emergency resettlement program in America's history. The program took place between May 1975 and December 1978. In this section I look particularly at the Vietnamese and Cambodian immigrants as they reflect two groups of people to be discussed in the new immigration wave novels.

The Vietnamese in the New Immigration Wave

The number of Vietnamese refugees in the United States grew rapidly between 1981 and 1992, and this group continues to be one of the nation's fastest-growing populations (Banks 1997). Many refugees in the 1975 wave represented an extension of the 1954 refugee movement in Vietnam. Many fled in fear of being caught up in the war that continued to rage in South Vietnam. The Indochina Migration and Refugee Act of 1975 granted parole to a maximum of 200,000 Vietnamese, Cambodian, and Laotian immigrants but did not set a limit for each representative group. Sixty-five percent of the refugees were Vietnamese (Banks 1997). The refugees could enter the United States if they met U.S. Immigration and Naturalization requirements, but they were not eligible to become permanent residents of the country.

Initially, only Vietnamese immigrants employed by the U.S. government and American companies operating in Vietnam were allowed to emigrate. This situation soon changed, as Vietnamese nationals from various parts of the country fought to be included in the evacuation process. Many of these refugees represented a different population than the American government had originally anticipated (Kelly 1977). Many immigrants arrived in large family units, that included extended family members. This sometimes proved problematic for sponsoring agencies which sought to divide them into smaller units to encourage sponsors to take them.

After settling in America, many Vietnamese nationals soon realized that they were no longer refugees but immigrants, as they realized they could not return to Vietnam. The resettlement process proved very difficult for many. Class positions played a major role in how the Vietnamese adapted to American customs. Those who had been high governmental officials, former managers, or the technical elite in Vietnam found themselves on equal footing with members of the lower-class nationals they had once ruled over (Kelly 1977). They lost their power, prestige, and income when they moved to the United States (Kelly 1977). To date, many Vietnamese immigrants have fought to improve their socioeconomic status in America. Their customs are also influencing American lifestyles.

The Cambodians in the New Immigration Wave

The Cambodian population makes up approximately two percent of the Asian-American population (Banks 1997). Cambodian refugees are among the recent arrivals in the new immigration wave. Before the large influx of refugees who fled their homeland to escape the Khmer wars arrived in 1975, Cambodians living in the United States came as settling immigrants, students, or Vietnamese nationals (Hopkins 1996). In her study of Cambodian refugees, Hopkins found that because of their recent arrival status there is not much written about the Cambodian experience in America, but she believes that this will change in the near future. Many may know of the refugee act that enabled Cambodians to enter the United States in 1975 and again in 1980 and 1981 but not much may be known or understood about their experiences here.

April 17, 1975 marked an unforgettable date in Cambodian history. This day was supposed to be the last day of the civil war and the beginning of a revolution (Chandler 1991). Instead, rebel forces called Red Khmers took over, drove the people from their homes into the countryside where they were forced to work as laborers, and killed many in the name of revenge. This inhumane treatment continued until 1978 and has been compared to the treatment of the Jews under Nazi rule (Chandler 1991). This experience explains why families fled their homes, many taking nothing with them, and sought refuge in the United States.

Today, many Cambodians who had to start from nothing are still struggling to survive and understand the new American culture to which they are exposed. Hopkins (1996) found that many people who have dealt with Cambodian refugees do not really "know" them. People judge them harshly because of their customs; for example, the way young girls wear makeup, without getting to know the refugees' traditions. Many adult Cambodians, even after living in the United States for fifteen years, still have limited knowledge of English. There is insufficient time for them to attend English classes because they have to go out and find work immediately to support their families. One important constant in these immigrants' lives is their strong sense of family. Hopkins asserts that more must be done for these displaced people to help them acclimate to American society. She argues that Cambodians want to be Cambodians first before they are forced to be Americans: "We leave little room in our social and ideological structures for individuals and states of ambiguity and transition, yet most refugees are in states of transition and need intermediate statuses to recognize and assist with that transition" (155). Refugees need to come to terms with their differing situations before they can be expected to grasp other experiences.

The experiences of the immigrants discussed in the new wave have varied, but there are similarities. Push factors force them to immigrate to the United States, and when they arrive, they have to acclimate to the way things are. Experiences such as that of the Cambodians illuminate the necessity for changes in how the needs of different groups are addressed in the new immigration wave.

Novels in the New Immigration Wave: 1965–Present

The new immigration wave novels reviewed in this section are *Journey of the Sparrows* (Buss 1991), *Children of the River* (Crew 1989), *Kim/Kimi* (Irwin 1987), *The Crossing* (Paulsen 1987), and *A Boat to Nowhere* (Wartski 1980). They are tales of children from El Salvador, Cambodia, Iowa, Mexico, and Vietnam, respectively. Each tale weaves a story that contributes to the way different immigrant groups, especially "minority immigrant populations," in the United States are regarded in the new immigration wave.

Synopses of the New Immigrant Novels

Buss, Fran L. (1991). *Journey of the Sparrows*. New York: Bantam Doubleday Dell. 155 pp.

Fifteen-year-old Maria, her older sister Julia, and their little brother Oscar are nailed into a crate with a young boy named Tomas and smuggled across the U.S.-Mexican border on the back of a truck into Chicago. There they struggle to survive along with other undocumented immigrants. As they try to find work to support themselves and send money back to their mother left behind in Mexico, they are always careful to remain "invisible" so they will not be arrested and deported by immigration officials. The burden of keeping the family together weighs heavily on Maria's shoulders, since Julia is pregnant. When their mother is arrested and deported back to El Salvador, Maria must make the terrifying journey alone back to Mexico to rescue their baby sister.

Crew, Linda. (1989). *Children of the River*. New York: Bantam Doubleday Dell. 213 pp.

Thirteen-year-old Sundara flees Cambodia with her aunt's family to escape the Khmer Rouge army. A church group in Oregon sponsors the family and they settle there. Sundara struggles to fit in with her American classmates and still remain "a good Cambodian girl" at home. When Sundara falls in love with an "all-American boy," her aunt is angry, believing that Sundara's relationship will bring disgrace to the family. Although she feels guilty about being disloyal to her past and her people's traditions, Sundara feels that her life should be different in America.

Irwin, Hadley. (1987). *Kim/Kimi*. New York: Puffin. 200 pp.

Although sixteen-year-old Kim shares a warm, loving relationship with her mother, stepfather, and half brother in an all-white Iowa community, she longs to find out about the Japanese-American father she never knew. Tired of being the object of disgust every time Japan's bombing of Pearl Harbor is discussed in her history class, and of always feeling like an outsider, she goes on a quest to solve her inner conflicts.

Traveling to California, she discovers events in Japanese-American history that were never mentioned in her history books or classes.

Paulsen, Gary. (1987). *The Crossing*. New York: Bantam Doubleday Dell. 114 pp.

Manny Bustos is an orphan scrounging to survive on the streets of Juarez, Mexico. During the day, he begs at restaurants or offers to help vendors in the food markets, hoping they will offer him something to eat. On the other side of the river is Sergeant Robert S. Locke, a Vietnam veteran who tries to stifle his memories of the Vietnamese war by drinking. Manny dreams of crossing the Rio Grande River, hoping for a better life in America. The two meet in a profound encounter.

Wartski, Maureen C. (1980). *A Boat to Nowhere*. New York: Signet. 152 pp.

Mai and her family thought they were safe from the war in their isolated Vietnamese village until Kien, a fourteen-year-old orphan, came into their lives bearing tales of terrible conquerors (the New Government) taking over villages. Soon the agents of the New Government arrived, bringing an end to the village's peace and happiness. Mai's grandfather is targeted for "reeducation" because he is a scholar. Kien helps the family to escape the tyranny of the conquerors. They become "boat people," risking the perils and dangers of the ocean in their desperate quest for freedom.

Individual Analysis of the New Immigrant Novels

Journey of the Sparrows by Fran L. Buss (1991)

***Race Representations in* Journey of the Sparrows.** Written in the first person, the story gives an intimate insight into Maria's experiences of being a refugee in the United States. The main characters in this novel are of Hispanic origin. They are either from El Salvador or Mexico and seemed willing to help each other acclimate as best they could.

Maria and her family endured an arduous journey crossing the Mexican border nailed in a crate. The family settled in Chicago, where they shared a small apartment with Alicia, a Salvadoran woman, and several Salvadoran men. Maria quickly realized the injustices of racism as she viewed how different people lived in her area. She pondered an issue that had bothered her even before her family was able to escape the vicious war.

Maria worried that America, a country that has so much, could be responsible for selling weapons to the guerrillas killing their own people in El Salvador. She worried that she had to try to be inconspicuous because America was unwilling to help Salvadoran refugees. Her father and brother-in-law were murdered in El Salvador, and the rest of the family feared the same fate awaited them if they were to go back home. How could "wonderful America" do this to poor people?

The inhumane treatment they received at the hands of those in charge of the American sweatshops is highlighted. At the shop where Maria was able to find work to help support her family, the workers had to be very careful because they had no idea when immigration officials would raid them. They were essentially at the mercy of greedy factory owners who wanted them to do the work but did not want to pay for their labor.

They had to work from dark to dark every day except Sunday for less than minimum wage. By the middle of the week, they went hungry because they had no money after paying the rent. The employers wanted them to do slave labor, but then they called in immigration authorities. Maria realized, "The boss had planned the raid so he wouldn't have to pay us. Tears scalded my cheeks, and I burned with fury" (69). Thus, the boss got his garments made with "free labor." Nobody in America seemed to care about that.

When Maria's sister, Julia, gave birth to a girl, Maria was happy that the baby would be an American citizen. She was excited at the prospect of being an aunt, but then the reality that the baby's life would be affected by racism hit her very hard. She worried that the baby was "so dark-skinned" (98). Although Maria had only been in America for a few months, she had already registered that the lighter the color of your skin, the more likely you were to get ahead. People with darker skin, even though they were not black, still had to worry about how they would fit into the American mainstream.

Maria was so bothered by the color of the baby's skin that she has great difficulty hiding her fears. She confided to Julia, "I'm afraid the baby's going to be dark, like me....She won't be beautiful. I'm thankful she's alive, but what if she looks like me?" (100). She did not think she was beautiful because her skin was not as white as Julia's. Since the baby's skin was also dark, Maria reasoned that she would also not be beautiful. Maria had already bought into the belief that to be beautiful in America, an individual has to have a light skin tone. In essence, the individual needs to be white.

***Class Representations in* Journey of the Sparrows.** Class representations were also very evident in this novel. Although the family did not immediately achieve any major socioeconomic improvements in their living conditions, they were constantly reminded of the life they left behind. They were so poor that all they had were "flowers and hunger" (4). The limited availability of food is still a constant companion in America as Maria reminisces about how poor they had been in El Salvador.

Amid the extreme poverty, however, her father's strength showed through. He and others fought to have a nurse in their village and to have their younger children learn to read. Even though he could not read, he still felt education was important. For this reason, her father and brother-in-law were killed and her sister was raped and left for dead.

Maria's recollection of the family's terrible ordeal back in El Salvador highlights for us that her experiences here in America are certainly not so horrific. After all, in America, no one has come after them to rape and kill them. So the immigration officials were called? That's not so bad. All the bad things she was recalling happened before she came to America.

Their socioeconomic status was obviously very low. They still slept in a room with several others, separated only by a curtain. When Maria lost her job at the garment factory, this created much hardship for the family, as food became scarce. Tomas, the young boy who crossed the border with them, soon found a church offering food to the poor. After drinking only water some days, the food was a welcomed blessing for the family. However, again this incident showed how much of a burden illegal immigrants can be. They are smuggled into the country but when they come, they cannot afford to support themselves. Churches and other caring organizations must bear the burden of supporting them.

Maria soon learned that their mother had been deported back to El Salvador, leaving their baby sister behind in Mexico in the hope that they would be able to rescue her. Maria realized that she would have to go back for the baby. The only problem was that the family had no money to finance the journey. Julia quietly decided that she would become a prostitute in order to get the money.

Issues of class representation can be viewed in two ways here. On the one hand, here is Julia, an older sister so concerned for the welfare of her younger sibling that she does not hesitate to do anything necessary to help. On the other hand, we see an illegal immigrant who has no scruples. She needs only an excuse to sell her body for money. Thankfully, with the help of friends who had little more than they did, Maria was able to go for her sister and Julia did not have to degrade her body.

Summary of Race and Class Representations in Journey of the Sparrows. Issues of both race and class representations were evident in the novel. Racial issues centered on the distinct separation of the Hispanic, or Latin American, community from other communities in the United States. For safety reasons, refugees stick together. Their landlord was white, but the only contact between them was when they paid their rent. Color is also important in their belief that people with "light" complexions had a better chance of succeeding in America.

Class issues are evident in that the people Maria and her family came in contact with were in the same situation. They cannot adopt mainstream values because they have to be careful of being found out. The belief that America is not so bad after all comes through. Why else would Maria risk her life to return to Mexico for her sister with the intention of bringing her back to Chicago? The impression is that the family's life may be bad in America, but it is a lot better than it was in El Salvador.

Children of the River by Linda Crew (1989)

Race Representations in Children of the River. Examples of Vietnamese and Cambodian immigrants highlight how different groups of people are treated as they are given the opportunity to settle in America. Sundara and her family, Cambodian refugees, had now been in America for four years, and the family had adjusted somewhat to the American lifestyle. Her uncle had finally started working as an accountant again, they had bought a new home, and the family owned two cars. Her family picked vegetables for the farmers, and her Aunt Soka tried hard to keep all the jobs in the family. However, another Chinese refugee family who came from Vietnam just moved into the community and was also determined to get as much work as they could.

Soka did not like the family's persistence, but she grudgingly acknowledged their determination to succeed. She always "pointed out with a grudging admiration, the Chinese could practically smell money to be made. You could not expect to keep work secret from them" (16). The Chinese family is depicted as a "money-grabbing" group of people. You can't hide anything from them. They will always find work wherever there is work to be had. This is one of the stereotypical images of the Chinese immigrant in America. It is fascinating that Soka held this view of them when she was also trying to keep all the jobs for her family.

Color seems to be a preoccupation for Sundara's family. Soka wanted her to be married into a respectable family, and education and color are two important qualifications for a husband. Soka saw the Vietnamese family's son as a good match for Sundara. If Sundara were to marry him, her "children would have whiter, prettier skin" (26). Soka was not happy that he was not Cambodian, but the fact that the children would have whiter skin made everything worthwhile. Of course, since they would have whiter skin, they would undoubtedly be prettier.

Sundara's preoccupation with the shade of her skin went further than her aunt's. When a young white "American" boy fell in love with her, his friends were convinced he was simply feeling sorry for her. After all, he was an "all-American" white male, the school's star quarterback, and the gem of a very well-to-do socialite family. When Jonathan invited her to his home, she broke the family tradition of not dating before the family arranges her marriage by going to visit. However, she was absorbed with how she thought the family saw her racial difference: "Sundara caught a glimpse of herself in the mirror...her hair was black, her skin darker than theirs? How strangely out of place she looked" (97).

While Jonathan's family seemed to be the perfect hosts, in that they seemed to genuinely take an interest in his new friend, Sundara's biggest concern was that her racial features were so obviously inferior. She was convinced that she looked out of place in the family's home.

While Soka was happy thinking about her niece marrying a man of Chinese racial origin, she was not so accommodating when she learned that Jonathan was interested in Sundara. After all, he was an "American." Of course, it goes without saying that an "American" is white. She asserted that no "good can come from going with Americans" (116). Soka temporarily changed her mind when she learned that Jonathan was the son of the highly esteemed doctor who saved her son's life when they had just arrived in America. However, she soon reverted to her earlier stubborn decision. Jonathan was white; therefore, they were different. He was not good enough, according to their family traditions.

Soka's strong dislike for the Americans soon dwindled as she learned that Jonathan's father was volunteering to work in a Cambodian refugee camp. When she first learned that the doctor wanted Sundara to teach him usable words in the Khmer language, she was suspicious that it was a ploy to get Jonathan and Sundara together. Her husband quickly convinced her otherwise. She conceded that it was hard to understand the Americans. "I have to admit, sometimes the Americans surprise me. Our upper-class Khmer people wouldn't *dream* of lowering themselves like that" (183). Here, an American was about to do something that people of the same stature in Cambodia would not have done because it would be beneath them.

Class Representations in Children of the River. Although Sundara's family was not considered among the elite in Cambodia, her family did well there. Her uncle worked for the U.S. government and they had a servant at home. When they settled in America, however, things changed. They could not afford a maid, and the family had to work hard as harvesters to supplement their income. Sundara's grandmother could not see beyond the fact that the family's socioeconomic status had changed for the worse. The reality that she probably would have been dead had they remained in Cambodia escaped her consciousness.

Sundara felt out of place because of the way she had to dress in America. Although the family rarely wore ethnic dress, the clothes they wore were mainly hand-me-downs from their sponsors. She yearned to be like the girls in school. Obviously, although she was concerned about her color, she also believed that if she dressed like the other girls (who were all white) she would fit in. Her socioeconomic status comes to the fore in that because the family had to work so hard for everything, they could not afford to buy "the finer things in life" like good clothes.

Class status again becomes the object of preoccupation as Sundara reminisced about the way life could have been had she been back in

Cambodia. She yearned for the normalcy she knew back then. In her yearning for life back home, however, Sundara forgot that the life of a debutante would not have been hers, as she was not considered a member of the upper class. Although life would be simpler back home, the status the family now enjoyed in America was more noble.

Summary of *Race and Class Representations in* Children of the River. The Cambodians are portrayed as conniving people who are concerned only about the welfare of their own. They are "hung up" on the issue of whiteness, believing that the lighter the color of your skin, the prettier you are. Race does play heavily into their beliefs. Although they like white skin, they prefer to mix with people who are more homogeneous to their racial makeup. They appreciate, to some extent, what the whites have done for them, but they do not want their relationship to go any farther.

Class issues were evident in the family's constant work ethic. In order to have a good life in America, they had to work long hours. They knew all the good places where vegetable harvesters were needed and they tried (Soka especially) to keep all the jobs for themselves. Soka is seen as greedy and conniving. She hates everything America stands for yet only in America could she speak on the same level with the wives of dignitaries from her homeland. In America her life has changed for the better, although you would never know this from the way she berates America. Soon, she brags about the benefits of becoming an American citizen. She is portrayed as an ungrateful person who is only here for what she can get!

Kim/Kimi by Hadley Irwin (1987)

Race Representations in Kim/Kimi. Of all the novels in the new immigration wave, this was the only one in which instances of racial representations predominate over class representations. Kim Andrews, born Kimi Yogushi, sets out on a quest to find out about her Japanese ancestry. Her Japanese-American father died when she was a baby and after her mother, a white woman, married a white man, her name was changed.

Kim became the object of racial discrimination at an early age. Her first exposure to her Japanese ancestry came at the hand of a spiteful classmate who often wanted Kim to allow her to cheat off her papers. When Kim did not oblige, the classmate called her a "dirty Jap" (11). Initially, she did not know what the term meant. As the years progressed, the discrimination became even more negative. She was overtly and covertly told that she was "different" from the other children in her ostensibly white neighborhood.

Kim became concerned that all her girlfriends were being invited to the movies by the boys in their group. She was the only one who was not invited. When she questioned why, her half brother, Davey, tells her, "You're different....Look in the mirror. You're Japanese" (39).

Obviously, because she was Japanese, none of the boys in her neighborhood could invite her out. Her own half brother found it incredible that she did not know why the boys refused to date her. It does seem strange, however, that the differences in her physical features were not explained to her by the people who mattered most, her parents.

Kim's physical features proved useful for her theatrical endeavors, although she never got the position she craved most. In her school programs, she was always considered for the role of an "oriental" character. Heidi, the classmate who called Kim a "dirty Jap," was considered the beauty in the class. She was blond and had a "very English" last name. Evidently, she was always chosen to play the lead roles.

Because of the treatment she received, Kim decides to go to California to find out about her father's family. Although she originally planned to go without telling any adult, her friend and younger brother told Mrs. Mueller, a retired teacher, who was sitting for Kim and Davey while their parents were away. Mrs. Mueller arranged for Kim to stay with a Japanese family, Barbara and her son Ernie.

Unfamiliar with Japanese-American customs, Kim fantasized about what she would discover when she met these people. She wondered if they all wore kimonos and black embroidered slippers. Would she have to take her shoes off when she entered their home, and would she be served raw fish and have to sit on the floor? She was shocked to see that Barbara and Ernie wore regular clothes and had a beautiful house. Barbara "could have been anybody's mother!" (71). Obviously, Kim had stereotypical conceptions of what a Japanese American looked like. Again, it does seem implausible that she knew nothing of the way Japanese Americans dress, live, and acclimate in American society.

Kim was unaware that the Japanese Americans had suffered a grave injustice when they were wrongfully detained in several camps after Japan bombed Pearl Harbor. She had learned about concentration camps in Germany but not about the plight of her ancestors in America. Her exposure to the Japanese-American culture proved to be very limited.

When Ernie took her to a party, Kim was amazed at the different races of people she saw. This was new to her. At home, she was the only nonwhite person in her school. At the party, "everybody was a different color…we were every shade you could imagine—From Minnie, a big woman with skin so black it almost glowed, to me" (115). While she could not understand why others thought she was "different," she quickly saw Minnie as an exotic creature. Kim saw herself as no different from the others, but obviously, this black woman's difference stands out. Here, again, another stereotypical image: that of the black person's exotic skin color.

When Kim's parents found out about her intention to go to California, they did not stop her. They knew it was something she had to do. Their "obvious love" for her seemed evident. They knew she was concerned about her Japanese ancestry and would not stand in the way of her going in search of her father's family. Again, I have to wonder why Kim had to go through this self-finding. Could her experiences have been different if her mother had spoken more openly to her about her father?

When Kim finally found her paternal family, she was at first scared about how they would receive her. At first she lied about who she was, and then she ran away in fear. When her family requested to see her again, she was at first surprised that her grandmother did not come out to see her. Kim later realized that her grandmother found it difficult to go against the wishes of her dead husband, that she should have nothing to do with their son because he had gone against the family's wishes and married a white American.

Although her grandmother could not yet release her uncertainties or go against her dead husband's wishes, she gave Kim a picture of her son as a young boy that she had kept secretly for years. Kim's aunt delivered the gift. "I felt my aunt draw near. 'Kenji!' she whispered. 'I didn't know Mother had this. Father made us destroy everything that belonged to my brother. She must have hidden this.' 'Will she let me see her?' My aunt rested her hand on my shoulder. 'She cannot, Kimi. Not yet. It is too soon for her—too soon and too late'" (199). There is hope yet!

Summary of Race and Class Representations in Kim/Kimi. The race issue was very dominant throughout this novel. There was not really a question of socioeconomic status in the story. Kim lived in a middle-class home; her mother gave her a credit card for emergencies. Her quest was more to discover why she looked different from her friends and to find those people who may look like her. The way racial representations were unveiled, though, is bothersome. Kim lived with her mother and stepfather, who were both white. Her mother was married to Kim's biological father, but he died in a car accident. It was difficult to understand why Kim was so ignorant of her Japanese connection. Could it be that her mother thought that Kim's life would be better if she did not know about her Japanese ancestry? Kim, then, is portrayed as an ungrateful child who has everything but is not satisfied. Her "difference" and quest to find out about that difference gives credence to the belief that she is an "outsider."

The Crossing by Gary Paulsen (1987)

Race Representations in The Crossing. Manny Bustos was an orphaned boy living on the streets. He was a prime target for crooks who captured young boys and sold them. Manny's physical features made his position even more dangerous. He had "red hair and large brown eyes with long lashes" (4). The crooks knew that they could get more money for Manny because his features set him apart from the other street children.

As he contemplated crossing to the United States, Manny knew how dangerous the attempt could be. The crooks, called street men, robbed people of their possessions, and they were the real danger that people attempting to cross feared. Manny knew that nothing could protect them from these dangerous street crooks. The Juarez police were too busy with their own problems, and the American police "or border patrol did not care if they were hurt or used or killed" (37). It would mean less illegal immigrants (undesirable Mexicans) to worry about.

When Manny met Sergeant Robert Locke, the boy saw his chance of getting to America. Something unexplainable drew him to the sergeant. Manny tried in every way to impress him. The mystique of the "American" did not escape Manny, even though he had not yet been to America. Manny believed that anything an American wants, an American gets. He tried to fulfill this for Robert by stealing a poster he saw the sergeant looking at.

The sergeant frequently crossed the border into Mexico. He had fought in the Vietnam War and was haunted by memories of his dead comrades. His only escape was to drown his sorrows by drinking. Manny realized that the sergeant drank a lot but is never really drunk. He finally confided that he wanted the sergeant to help him emigrate to America. However, on a fateful night, as the sergeant prepared to return to the United States, Manny was attacked by the street men and the sergeant tried to protect him.

The sergeant, in an unselfish show of bravery, defended the homeless boy but ended up being killed. Of course, with his strong military training, he managed to kill the street men before succumbing to his injuries. In a last show of bravery, the sergeant gave Manny his wallet and told him to run to the United States and make something of himself. "'Take it,' Robert said now. 'Take it and run and cross and get the green card and live there. It is what you want. What I want you to have'" (114). While Manny wavered, the sergeant told him to get out before the police arrived. The sergeant died before he was able to say anything else but the good deed was done. A kind white sergeant had given his life for an orphaned Mexican boy.

***Class Representations in* The Crossing.** Manny's homelessness caused much pain. He constantly had to fight to survive on the streets and because of his small stature he was an easy target for the bigger boys. He was determined to change his circumstances by going to America. Manny was awed by the way Mexicans living in America came home all dressed up. They wore leather belts with large buckles and straw hats with feathers. He was convinced that an improved socioeconomic status meant having these distinguished accessories.

While he wished for a better life in America, the realities of home proved too strong for Manny to ignore. He was constantly hungry and often went to bed without eating. He had to fight for food, and even when someone was kind enough to feed him, it was never enough. This constant hunger was more than enough to cause Manny to dream of life in the United States.

Manny's grandest meal came one day thanks to Sergeant Locke. As the sergeant entered a hotel Manny was normally chased out of, he followed behind hoping to get something to eat. When the waiter tried to chase him away, the sergeant told him to bring Manny in. As the waiter reluctantly gave the boy a menu, Manny knew his hunger would be abated at least for the day.

While Manny was happy for the free meal, his intense hunger showed through. He could not read the menu but requested every food item he knew from memory. He avoided the sergeant's eyes for fear that the man would change his mind about buying the meal. He was so unaccustomed to a restaurant meal that when he got one, he asked for everything edible he had possibly dreamed about on those hungry days when he had nothing to eat.

Summary of Race and Class Representations in The Crossing. This novel is another prime example of some of the push factors that drive people to desperate measures to seek asylum in the United States. It also gives credence to the notion that America has nothing to do with the experiences some of these people encounter in their countries of origin. America is not to be blamed for anything bad that happens in another country. After all, an American gave his life so Manny, a homeless orphan, could get the chance to come to America.

Manny was a very lucky boy whose misfortunes turned out for the good. Unfortunately, the good comes at the expense of an "American." An American soldier, no less. Although many blame America for its treatment of Mexican immigrants, there are Americans who willingly make sacrifices to help them.

A Boat to Nowhere by Maureen C. Wartski (1980)

Race Representations in A Boat to Nowhere. As the war raged in Vietnam, people in small hidden villages were able to escape its travesties. However, when the New Government took charge, these small villages were soon targeted to "help the government." Mai's was one such village. When representatives for the New Government arrived in the village they accused Thay Van Chi, Mai's grandfather and the leader of the village, of treason because he was educated, and they burned all his books. Aided by the orphan Kien, Grandfather and his grandchildren, Mai and Loc escaped. They traveled to Thailand, where Grandfather had told them the people were friendly and would take them in. When they arrived in Thailand, however, they were not allowed to go ashore but were treated with hostility instead.

Tired of the many refugees seeking asylum in their country, the Thais turned the family away. With no other option, the family became boat people, hoping to head to Malaysia. At sea, they faced many obstacles: storms, pirates, and ships whose captains refused to pick them up simply because they knew they were Vietnamese. One sailor rationalized, "No country wants those refugees anyway, and we can't support them all, can we?" (99). Obviously, at sea, the refugees were discriminated against solely because of who they were. Since no country wanted them, they were left on the treacherous ocean to die.

After many dangerous days at sea, the family was spotted by an American ship. Unfortunately, help came too late for Grandfather. He died at sea and the three children had to throw his body overboard. As the children were rescued, however, Kien recognized that the rescuers were Americans. Before he drifted into an unconscious state he acknowledged, "You...friend? Okay?... Take care of my brother and sister," he whispered brokenly in Vietnamese. "They are sick" (148). Kien knew that with the coming of the Americans, they would now be safe. While everyone else turned them away, even their own, the Americans would take them to safety. The Americans were their friends.

One sailor, angered by the children's experiences, certainly fulfilled Kien's belief. He determined that even if he had to be their sponsor, he would ensure that they received asylum in the United States. Although the family did not set out to come to America, this was the country that ultimately saved them, with no strings attached.

***Class Representations in* A Boat to Nowhere.** When the representatives for the New Government discovered their village, the villagers knew things would never be the same again. Kien, a homeless boy who had escaped from other villages conquered by the messengers, had warned Grandfather that they would come eventually; now they had.

Although they were already poor, the villagers knew that they would be expected to give something to the government. They knew that they had no choice in the matter. Everything was supposed to be for the good of the government. They should be honored to help the government in every possible way.

Curious to know the percentage that would be required for the government, Grandfather inquired while the villagers waited uneasily for the response. He was upset to learn that they would have to give fifty percent of their earnings to the government. Seeing that Grandfather resisted them at every turn, the representatives sought to find something to blame him for. When they discovered his scholarly books, they determined that he should apologize to the people for what he had taught them. Obviously, they did not appreciate anyone who did not share their views. Once honored as a learned scholar, his own countrymen were now treating him as if he were a traitor to their country.

***Summary of Race and Class Representations in* A Boat to Nowhere.** This book was effective in describing the experiences of people in their own countries. While it offers a reason for why people immigrate, it also presents a picture of how uncaring other people can be to these people's plight. Race was evident in the way this family was turned away from Thailand. Because they were Vietnamese refugees, the Thais did not want them to come ashore. Race also came out in the negative way the sailor, on the first ship that spotted the family, reacted to seeing these desperate people at sea. The Americans are portrayed as kind, loving people who will do anything for strangers, simply because they care.

Combined Analysis of the Novels
in the New Immigration Wave: 1965–Present

The stories relating experiences of immigrants in the new wave depict various groups of "minority status" immigrants represented in the history of this time period.

Who Are the Immigrants?

Although the novels in the new immigration wave share an important characteristic in that they all relate tales of immigrants currently regarded as "minority" populations in the United States, each story is also very distinct in its relating. Of the five novels, four of the protagonists are females: Maria in *Journey of the Sparrows,* Sundara in *Children of the River*, Kim in *Kim/Kimi*, and Mai in *A Boat to Nowhere.* The fifth protagonist is Manny, the young boy in *The Crossing.* Of the five novels, Kim's character is the only one that does not reflect a recent immigrant's story, as she was born in Iowa. It is important to note that she does travel across state lines to find out about her Japanese heritage.

Where Do They Come From?

The novels in the new immigration wave represent people from different nations. Maria in *Journey of the Sparrows* is a Salvadoran refugee who sought refuge in Mexico. From there, she and her family were smuggled across the border and to Chicago. Sundara in *Children of the River* is a Cambodian refugee living in Oregon. She fled the Khmer wars with her aunt's family. Kim in *Kim/Kimi* is a Japanese American living in Iowa, but she went on a quest to California to find out about her Japanese-American ancestry. Mai in *A Boat to Nowhere* is a Vietnamese refugee who, with her grandfather, brother, and friend Kien, escaped the New Government as they became boat people in search of a new home and freedom. Finally, Manny in *The Crossing* is a young Mexican orphan with dreams of making America home.

What Are Their Experiences Before and After They Came?

Before Experiences. The before experiences portrayed in the novels are similar for some of the characters. In *Journey of the Sparrows*, Maria came from a poor area where wars ravaged the land and everyone who could escaped in search of a better life. Maria, her mother, older sister, and two younger siblings escaped after her father and brother-in-law were killed by the Guardias.

In *Children of the River*, Sundara and her family escaped at the onset of the Khmer takeover of Cambodia. While the family was not considered elite, her uncle worked for the American government and the family lived comfortably.

In *Kim/Kimi*, Kim came from a middle-class family in a predominantly white neighborhood in Iowa. Both her mother and stepfather were white and Kim was raised in a "white" cultural environment. As she was more overtly reminded that she is different because of her Japanese-American ethnicity, Kim determined to find out more about her biological father and his family.

Mai in *A Boat to Nowhere* lived in a small but industrious village in Vietnam. The village was so secluded that the people were sheltered from any knowledge of the war ravaging their land. When they were finally discovered by government agents, Mai's family escaped with hopes of finding freedom.

Manny, the young boy in *The Crossing*, was an orphan living in Mexico. He lived in poverty on the streets and struggled daily to survive. His biggest dream was to come to America where he could work and obtain the basic necessities of life.

After Experiences. Various occurrences helped to shape the later experiences of the five protagonists. After arriving in Chicago, Maria in *Journey of the Sparrows* struggled along with her pregnant sister to take care of their younger brother. They also sent money to Mexico to help their mother, who had remained behind with the youngest sibling, who was sick. Maria experienced an immigration raid at the sweatshop she worked in, but she escaped without being seen. Being a gifted artist, Maria sold a few of her paintings but does not make much money to support the family. With the help of a minister, she found a few days' work and the church helped with food.

Sundara in *Children of the River* learned firsthand how different life was in the United States as her family adjusted to living in America. The family did well, however, and after four years they owned their own home and two cars. At school, Sundara tried to fit in but her heavy accent and Asian features caused her to stand out. She worried about her dark complexion and found it difficult to believe that a young "American" boy, the school star, liked her.

In *Kim/Kimi*, as Kim went on her quest to discover her Japanese-American roots, she realized that most of the images she had of Japanese Americans were stereotypical. She found that the people she visited did much the same things she did, wore the same types of clothes, and were simply regular folks. There was nothing exotic about them. When she located her father's family, her grandmother found it hard to handle the realization that she had a granddaughter. Her son had married a white woman without the family's permission, and after all these years that reality was still painful. While she needed time to grasp all that had happened, she gave Kim some hope that she would talk to her one day.

In *The Crossing*, Manny had not yet made it to America, but there was the strong implication that he would. For Manny, the story was very sad. The one person he depended on most, Sergeant Robert Locke, was killed by Mexican street men as he tried to protect his young friend. The future seemed bright for Manny, however, when, as he lay dying, the sergeant handed Manny his wallet and told him to run on to the United States and fulfill his wishes.

Mai in *A Boat to Nowhere* also now had hopes of coming to America after she and the others are rescued by an American ship. One of the sailors, on seeing the poor health of the three children, determined that even if he had to do it himself, he would ensure that they got asylum in the country. After the ghastly journey at sea, this was the greatest hope for these children.

How Are Issues of Race and Class Represented in the Novels?

The critique of race and class representations conducted in the first section of the analysis of the new immigration wave novels speaks specifically to the main and subquestions of this section.

How Are Characters Racially Identified?

The protagonists in the new immigration novels are all members of racial groups identified as minority (or nonwhite) populations in the United States today: Asians and Hispanics. Like the immigrants of the early and middle immigration waves, who were distinguished by where they came from, the characters in these novels are racially identified according to their country of origin.

Are Issues of Race and Class Present in the Novels?

Instances of race representations of immigrants were identified in all five novels, while class representations were obvious in all but *Kim/Kimi*. Each book addressed different aspects of race and class according to the context of each story. One thing that seemed constant, however, was that each individual was an outsider.

In *Journey of the Sparrows*, the racial representation of the immigrants was overt. The Salvadoran characters were all undocumented immigrants. The only people who lent support to them were two older women of Hispanic origin who were born in America. Unlike the other refugees (the Cambodians and the Vietnamese), who had sponsors and were being aided by these sponsoring organizations, the Salvadorans quite noticeably were fighting for survival on their own. Their class status was very low. Since the parents were absent, this promises to be another undocumented family who will ultimately depend on financial support from the government. Although they had made it to America, Maria and her family were still the outsiders. They had to be careful about everything because at any moment they could be deported back to their war-torn country.

In *Children of the River*, Sundara had settled into a comfortable life-style. Her family was sponsored by an organization and after four years, their class status had improved remarkably. However, their racial back-ground still made them the "other." While they seemed to have been brought into the mainstream culture, there was still the reminder that they were different. Racial representations, however, seem to be the preoccupation of the immigrants rather than the Americans. Soka worried about Sundara having "whiter-skinned" children when she got married, while Sundara's main concern was that her dark color makes her feel out of place with Jonathan's "American" family. Her features were compared to a "Hawaiian Princess," a feature the American vegetable farmer relished as she sold his produce at the Saturday market. Her status improved as she saved to buy a new winter coat and the kind of clothes worn by her American classmates.

In *Kim/Kimi*, Kim was bothered by racial issues. Presumably since her parents were white, her financial status did not bear questioning. However, although she had grown up without any positive exposure to her Japanese-American heritage, Kim was reminded by others around her (white classmates and friends) that she was not white. As she traveled to California to unearth her ancestry, she was bogged down with negative stereotypes of what a Japanese American would be like. Kim quickly fell in love with everything Japanese but she soon realized how little she really knew about the culture.

Manny, the young boy in *The Crossing*, faced racial oppression because of his unusual physical characteristics. He was the constant target of street thugs and was expected to fetch a higher price because of his hair color and the length of his eyelashes. His greatest enemy was class-related. He was an orphan who hunted for food on the streets, begging at restaurant doors and anywhere someone would not chase him away. His constant dream of coming to America, of being a man with nice belts, shoes, and hats, is evidence of how badly he wanted to improve his socioeconomic status.

Although the characters in *A Boat to Nowhere* were not rich, they lived comfortably farming and taking care of every individual in their village. Everyone cared about each other's welfare, and Thay Van Chi, Mai's grandfather, taught every villager to read and about the world outside their village. Racial representations come to the fore as the family sought asylum in other countries and were turned away because nobody wanted to be crowded by Vietnamese boat people. The people who ultimately rescued them were the "white savior" Americans, who could not believe the "injustices" these people had faced in their lives. Class issues are evident in the way the people in Vietnam were treated by their own countrymen. Everyone was expected to accept living under a dictatorship. Those who protested were treated like the enemy.

Do These Images Change for Different Immigrant Groups?

The images presented of the different immigrant groups indicate levels of differences in the five novels. The way they were treated had varying degrees. Maria, the Salvadoran, and Manny, the Mexican, were both Hispanic immigrants. Both fell under the undocumented immigrant label and their socioeconomic status in America did not promise to be much improved. They would be stuck working in a sweatshop or on a farm and would become new beneficiaries of the welfare system. Also very evident is the fact that they had limited exposure to formal education.

Kim, the Japanese American, did not pose a problem since she was the daughter of a successful white middle-class family. Her major concern was with finding out about her birth father's family; essentially, finding out about the side of her that made her different. She was not bothered by constant hunger or low-class status. She did not have to work to support herself and the family. She had a credit card for emergency spending. Unlike the lives of all the other characters, her life is highly representative of that of the ideal American, and to a large degree, that of the Asian-American immigrant in America.

Sundara's life had been better than the Hispanics. While she had to work to help the family, her life was not filled by the constant drudgery of poverty and hunger. The family was sponsored by an organization; thus, they were acclimated into life in America and were helped along the way. They did not have to hide like Maria and her family, working without pay because their employers called immigration on them. In five years, they would be eligible to apply to become U.S. citizens. Mai's life promises to be similar to Sundara's. She too would be sponsored so her life would not be the cat-and-mouse game it had been for Maria and Manny.

How Are Different Immigrant Groups Presented?

The Hispanic immigrants are poor and have to "sneak" into the country. They join the long list of undocumented immigrants who stretch the resources of the government. The Japanese American does not pose a problem because she is from a good family. Now that she has found out about her Japanese-American ancestry, she can return home and go back to being the "loving daughter" who tries to improve her school grades. Sundara, another Asian immigrant, shows strong promise of being successful. She is very smart and hopes to win a full college scholarship to become a doctor. Mai, also an Asian immigrant, will be sponsored so her life promises to be similar to Sundara's.

How Do Characters Handle Cross-Cultural Encounters?

Each character dealt with cross-cultural interactions differently. For Maria, cross-cultural encounters came in the form of other Hispanics, namely Mexicans. Since they shared a common language and immigration status, she got along well with them. Although she did not have an entourage of friends, Sundara seemed to have positive cross-cultural experiences. She did well in school and was respected by her teachers. Her only immediate enemy was Jonathan's ex-girlfriend, a white all-American cheerleader. She enjoyed American foods and customs, so her aunt accused her of being more American than Cambodian. Kim realized that she enjoyed the Japanese-American customs and felt that she fit in well.

Historical Evaluation of New Immigration Novels

Although the novels exhibited many instances where the issues of race and class presented negative representations of immigrants in the new wave, these representations also served to highlight the different levels of acceptance of immigrants from different racial backgrounds. The experiences of different immigrant groups in this period were discussed at the beginning of the chapter.

Since Kim was born and raised in America, and due largely in part to her family's background, her experiences are very different from the others in this period. Her lack of exposure to the Japanese-American culture and to the socioeconomic status Japanese Americans have attained in America, and her ignorance of the way people of this race were treated back in the 1940s, all demonstrate how sheltered Kim's life had been. While Kim experienced racial problems, they were on a small scale in comparison with the others. For her, the travesties of war were only a recollection of others' lived experiences.

Maria's experiences are consistent with those described in the historical analysis. She came from a poor country and was not warmly welcomed into the United States; thus, she resorted to the desperate measure of being smuggled in. Although she had arrived in America, her status as an undocumented immigrant indicates that she would still live in poverty. The little money Maria and Julia were able to make had to supplement their living expenses here, and they also had to send a portion to help their mother left behind in Mexico. One positive factor for Maria is that unlike many other Salvadoran refugees, including her sister, she learned to read and write before she immigrated. This proved very beneficial for her.

Sundara's family was helped in their relocation; thus, the process was not as daunting for them. As the historical data describes, sponsoring agents assisted in helping them to get settled, providing them with room and board and helping them to secure jobs. They were able to succeed with this help and soon were regarded on the same level with people who would have been their superiors in Cambodia. Their immigration to America proved beneficial to their socioeconomic status. Their ability to achieve in America was limited only by their imaginations.

Although they had not yet arrived, the differences between Manny and Mai are also very obvious. While the sergeant gave Manny his wallet before he died so that the boy could go to America, Manny's prospects are not certain. He might make it across the border or he might not. If he does, he will be an undocumented immigrant like Maria, and the money in the sergeant's wallet can only last for a limited time. Mai, on the other hand, promises to have a future much like Sundara's. She will be aided by refugee acts passed to assist refugees from Vietnam, and life for her will not have to start where Maria's and Manny's begin.

The obvious levels of difference do come to the fore. The immigrants in the new wave are members of "minority" groups. They are the "new" immigrants, the "outsiders" or the "thems." While they all fit under the "minority" classification, they are in no way regarded as being the same. Immigration laws provide asylum for some while others have to forage in order to stay alive. The ways that different groups are treated demonstrate how their acclimation to American mainstream culture will be.

The novels in this period portray the Asian experience in a positive light, while the Hispanic experience does not seem as promising. The portrayals also highlight for us that the more people are helped at the initial stages of immigrating, the less likely they are to become public charges of the government. Also, while many nativists today feel that immigrants come only to live off the government, the stories indicate that immigrants do work (even if they are in danger of being deported and not getting paid) to support themselves and also to send money back to their countries of origin to help other family members who have not been able to leave. Many of these immigrants risk everything in hopes of gaining some sense of the "American dream." They work hard in many menial jobs that others refuse to do, hoping to earn enough to support their families. Without the help of kind citizens, many remain in obscurity for years, never gaining legal residency.

Chapter 6

Dominant Race and Class Representations of Immigrants in Children's Literature

> We have had far too much immigration in far too few years. We need to ask basic questions: Are we still trying to fill up an empty continent? Does the United States face an acute labor shortage? We have no need for immigration today.
>
> - Dan Stein, executive director of For American Immigration Reform "FAIR" in an interview with *American Legion Magazine* 1995, 26

Finally, I return to the above epigraph, which was introduced at the beginning of this book, to interrogate the issues of race and class representations in children's literature. I began in Chapter 1 with a discussion of how immigration has influenced the making of the United States, looking at the current discomfort with recent immigration. I wanted to find out how widespread Stein's forceful sentiment on the issue of immigration was and if this same sentiment was evident in earlier immigration periods.

Stein's argument suggests that immigrants are people who come to the United States only to fill empty land spaces and to alleviate labor shortages. From his argument, it would be difficult to determine that people regarded as "Americans" today are actually descendants of immigrants. I discovered that Dan Stein's contention—that America no longer needs immigrants because it is no longer an empty continent needing to be filled—illuminates a strong sentiment that has plagued (and still is plaguing) American history from the early eighteenth century. This discovery was clearly revealed in this study by a critical analysis of the novels and the three historical immigration waves.

Patrick's (1986) assertion that stirring stories about immigrants contribute to our country's image as a symbol of hope, freedom, and opportunity proved true for some characters whose lives in America turned out for the best, but untrue for others who did not find their future prospects to be so hopeful. For this latter group, the representational image of immigrants proves to be negative. Nelkin (1995) ascertains that this type of negative treatment has always been present in America's history. Immigrants in this category (like the Mexican and Salvadoran immigrants) were easily dismissed by others around them as they struggled to survive in America.

In his discussion of how people from "dominant" and "non-dominant" groups are treated differently, Courts (1997) asserts that "the dominant Discourse in any society has the power to bury the non-dominant voices (and bodies) of those who do not share that Discourse" (72). The Mexican and Salvadoran immigrants discussed here do fit into this non-dominant group. They do not share the power or discourse of dominant groups, thus their experiences are commonly treated with little respect.

Shannon (1994) argues that "we are all cultural beings who should acknowledge the biased cultural basis of all history, who should recognize the political, oppressive intent of those who use labels such as 'normal' or 'patriot' to dismiss social groups" (5). For many of the immigrant groups discussed in this study, the "biased cultural basis" proves only too true. Unfortunately, our recollection of America's history, and the roles these people play in that history, often leaves us in a state of "historical amnesia" (Macedo 1994: 11) as we tend to have selective recollection about the historical foundations and continued expansion of the United States.

Issues of immigration have been widely debated in the media in recent years. People have been insistent that the government needs to do something to stop the huge influx of immigrants coming in, especially of undocumented immigrants. The drastic measure taken by California when it passed Proposition 187, a bill that denies support to undocumented immigrants and their children, emphatically demonstrates that many Americans are fed up with immigration and want it to be stopped or limited.

This study is grounded in the belief that race and class representations have always been present in the immigration debate. Americans have always expressed an intolerance with immigrants, especially if they are not of the same racial, ethnic, or socioeconomic backgrounds as themselves. As early as the 1800s, newly arriving immigrants were discriminated against because of the countries they emigrated from; how their forefathers were treated in their countries of origin; the way they spoke; their religious affiliations; and more important, the color of their skin. These continued negative experiences indicate for us that racism in America must be fought in all ways possible and by all who are concerned about how it affects us as a people (Delpit 1992). So, too, class discrimination should be obliterated.

The undertaking of this book was important for several reasons: I wanted to find out how these issues of race and class were portrayed in relation to different immigrant populations in the United States, and I felt that unearthing their portrayal would shed light on some of the present discontent with immigrants. Since race and class issues are evident in what is said, or not said, in historical recordings, I wanted to see how these issues were, or were not, addressed in the literature. Finally, I think that the study of immigration was important because it looks at an issue that has been an integral ingredient in the making of the United States of America. I believe that gleaning an understanding of how issues of immigration have been handled over the years illuminates the reasons for current debate on the subject.

Reading makes immigrants of us all as it takes us away from home and finds homes for us everywhere (Rochman 1993). Good books help to break down cultural barriers. They dissipate prejudice and build community. Good books should help students develop their awareness of the world around them (Courts 1997). Literature has always been important in people's lives. It is a medium of representation used with children in classroom settings and many times presents views that children would not otherwise experience. Literature is a vital resource that helps us to navigate our way through past and present views of who we are and who we might become as members of a diverse society (Enciso 1994). It is one means of passing down traditions from one generation to another, and once a tradition is written down, it is not as dependent on human memory as the spoken word. It is a form that lasts when the keepers of the spoken word have gone.

Because of the obvious continued presence of the written word, I felt that this study was important in that it looks at works about immigrants that relate experiences from different immigration periods and compares these experiences to gain a better understanding of how, and why, immigrants are viewed the way they are in the United States. However, as the discussion throughout this study indicates, literature must be viewed through critical lenses to query the types of messages they impart to readers.

Scholars and others involved in the development of young minds have always struggled over the content of children's reading materials (Shannon 1992). While this study does not seek to censor any reading material, I deliberately examined these novels to see the types of messages that are being transmitted to children. Children need to explore literature from various points of view (Courts 1997). Courts further asserts that "wrong things have been done throughout history and continue to be done; the Holocaust, slavery, the devastation of Native Americans, the invasion of Mexico, the abuse of Chinese labor on the rail-roads, the mistreatment of Irish....All these things actually occurred and are part of our history" (145). The point then is not to censor these representations in books but rather to deal with these sensitive issues in an educationally systematic way.

Macedo (1994) argues that children must be allowed to question dominant views presented to them. They are not empty vessels waiting to be filled. Like adults, children need to be critical thinkers. He posits that when children are not allowed to be critical, they are being given "education for domestication," a type which "borders on stupidification" and "provides no pedagogical space" for them to grow (18). In order for children to become critical thinkers, they need to have teachers who are critical thinkers (Kincheloe 1993), who will lead the way for them.

Critical Literacy: Race and Class Representations in Literature

To achieve the purpose of this study, a thematic content analysis technique was used. This was done based on a critical literacy and sociology of literature theoretical framework. I incorporated the following beliefs: there are no absolutes; literature always represents or reflects something else; representations are not innocent (Kincheloe 1997); authors write books that are highly reflective of their social environments; authors do not operate in a vacuum; they make choices about how they represent the world; and finally literature is directly related to our social lives (Hall 1979). In order to see this direct relation, a thorough investigation requires that we do not accept everything as a given but rather that we critically evaluate those issues placed before us (Kincheloe and McLaren 1994).

With four main questions directing the study, the individual analyses in Chapters 3, 4, and 5 centered on the first three questions: What are the common images of immigrants?, how are issues of race and class represented?, and how do these images change for different immigrant groups? The fourth question, not yet addressed, is: Do images of race and class change for different time periods? The remainder of this chapter is intended in part to answer the specifics of this question, to offer a final analysis and assessment of the history of immigration in the United States, and to discuss how educators may use these novels to develop students' understanding of the complexities of the myths and stories about immigrants in the United States.

Race and Class Representations
in the Three Immigrant Waves: 1820–Present

Do Race and Class Representations Change for Different Time Periods?

The immigration periods were divided into three waves: 1820–1899, 1900–1964, and 1965–present. Seventeen books relating the experiences of immigrants in the three waves were analyzed. This question is intended to explore the changes in race and class representations of immigrants portrayed in the novels analyzed across the three focused immigration periods. The broader question of changes in race and class representations was broken into smaller focus questions to look specifically at: Are novels reflective of the historical periods they represent? And how are images of immigrants represented across the three immigrant periods? This section will address these two sub-questions before the larger question of changes is addressed.

Are Novels Reflective of the Historical Periods They Represent?

The novels in the three immigration waves were reflective of the immigrant populations represented in the historical data discussed in this study. The four books in the early immigration wave related tales of immigrant children from Bohemia, Ireland, Africa, and Native Americans in Arizona. The eight books in the middle immigration wave related tales of immigrant children from Russia, Germany, Poland, Ukraine, and China. Finally, the five books in the new immigration wave related tales of children from El Salvador, Cambodia, a Japanese American in Iowa, Mexico, and Vietnam.

The way in which these different immigrant groups traveled to the United States and tried to adapt to life here is reflective of how both dominant and alternative forms of history relate them. For example, the earlier immigrants came by boat and landed in New York, where they underwent various tests if they were poor. The tests were before they would be admitted into the United States. The later immigrants came by airplane, boat, foot, and car, and passed through different immigration ports across the states. In the historical discussion of each immigration wave, facts on how different groups came to the United States were discussed. Across the three waves, immigrants came because of religious freedom (for example, the Jews), socioeconomic crises in their homelands (for example, the Irish), and wars and other driving forces that caused them to seek a new life in the United States (for example, the Cambodians and Vietnamese).

The representations of the immigrants in the three immigrant waves were reflective to a certain degree of the historical periods they repre- sented. The images presented of them, however, were predominantly negative representations that, for the most part, gave no explanations of why circumstances were as they were. Although the history relates tales of how earlier immigrants who had become "Americans" fought against other immigrants coming in and the legislative laws proved that only certain classes of people would be accepted, for the most part, the stories portrayed tales of the immigrants being worried about issues that ultimately did not affect their success in America.

Issues of race and class were identified in all books but most did not set the historical context of these two issues deeply. For example, in *The Slave Dancer* the captain is portrayed as the cruel boss who buys slaves for profit. He is upset at the British ships protecting the waters to prevent greedy folks from bringing more slaves to the West. The British are portrayed as the good guys when they were the ones who actually started the process of transporting and selling slaves. Very few references to the structural racism and classism issues, as they were brought out in the study, were made as each author wove tales of immigrants' experiences in the United States.

Generally, the stories implied that the problems faced by immigrants happened because of individuals acting without structural backing. For example, in *The Star Fisher*, the only overt experiences with racism that the Lees had came at the hand of a town "bum" and his friend. The townspeople are seen as good people who only needed a little prodding from Miss Lucy to show how very hospitable they really were. While the stories related experiences that were common across the novels, I got the sense that you could easily point fingers at the "few bad apples" who caused or instigated problems for the immigrants, as the Lees' case suggested.

How Are Images of Immigrants Represented Across the Three Immigrant Periods?

Most of the immigrants in the novels are portrayed as people who came to America only to benefit from the vast riches that the country has to offer. They came simply to enhance their personal lifestyles in a country that gave them the "freedom" to do as they pleased. For example, the Chinese immigrants came in search of the "golden mountains"; the Jews came because of religious freedom; the Irish and the Mexicans came because of socioeconomic crises. This, of course, was not true for the Africans, who were involuntarily brought here as slaves.

Very little is said about the value these different immigrant groups have added to making America the country it is today. They are not portrayed as contributors to the enhancement of the country's welfare. However, many of these immigrants were needed, and were oftentimes exploited, for cheap labor. Railroads, manufacturing companies, garment industries, agriculture, and domestic jobs are only a minute fraction of how these people have helped to make America the country it is today.

The predominant image of the immigrants portrays how good life in America could be for them. Many immigrants who were very poor in their homeland (for example, the Polish immigrants in *The Cat Who Escaped from Steerage*) came with high hopes of becoming rich in America. While the Jews suffered religious and racial prejudice in their homelands, when they arrive in America their experiences are generally positive. With hard work (no problems with racial and religious problems here) they are able to quickly overcome their initial poverty and soon bask in the riches America offers. The Irish immigrants also become Americans and their initial position as domestic workers is quickly forgotten. The Asians, although there may be singular instances of racism, also quickly enjoy an American experience that enables them to get their piece of the American "pie." These success stories imply that immigrant experiences that conflict with these images happen only because of something the immigrants did. Otherwise, negative experiences were the push factors that brought them here in the first place.

The immigrants discussed in this study experienced varying degrees of racial and socioeconomic discrimination in the three immigration waves. While the images of the different groups shared some similarities, their overall representation differed across the three immigrant periods. The analyses of the novels showed that images were different within the individual periods as well as across the periods. Differences in treatment came across in different themes: Immigrants who came with both parents were more likely to succeed in the United States than those immigrants who came alone or with only one parent; white immigrants were more likely than nonwhite immigrants to succeed and assimilate into American mainstream culture by simply working hard.

The patterns that emerge from the three immigration waves indicate that in the early immigration wave, the problems of racism and classism mainly occurred here in the United States. Many people left their homelands in search of better future prospects as they boarded ships bound for America. Racial discrimination increased when white Europeans, fearing that nonwhite immigrant groups were benefiting financially, created discriminatory laws to keep these later immigrant groups out.

In the middle immigration wave, however, most of the instances of race and class discrimination began in the immigrants' countries of origin and were the push factors that caused them to immigrate to America. Thus, America was not responsible for the discrimination they experienced. Instead, America was the welcoming country that took them in and sheltered them from the miseries inflicted by their own countrymen.

Finally, in the new immigration wave, the immigrants seem particularly concerned with identity issues. America is depicted as a very structured and completely developed country. The immigrants in this period have problems fitting into American culture, not because of anything America does to them but because of their self-discrimination. They see themselves as "different" and as "outsiders"; thus, in order to form solidarity, they resort to championing their individual identities. They are unlike many early and middle immigration wave immigrants who changed their names and customs to blend in with others as they assimilated into the dominant culture. The new immigrants' preoccupation with their identity causes them to stick with people of their own racial and ethnic backgrounds. They do not live up to the "melting pot" image that America portrays to the outside world.

Do Race and Class Representations Change for Different Time Periods?

To answer the general question of whether race and class representations differ for the three immigration waves, the summaries of the two sub-questions highlight that the representations do change for different time periods in some ways but remain the same in others. People who are different in racial and socioeconomic status from the dominant population are always treated differently. They are the "outsiders" or the "other." Many are always defined or identified more by who they are and where they originated rather than on the contributions they have made to help make the United States the country it is today. In order to address this question of representation across the novels in more depth, the immigrants were divided by racial origin and by socioeconomic level.

The categories that developed as the study progressed are: Africans; Asians; Native Americans; South Americans (Latin Americans/Hispanics); whites (Western and Eastern Europeans); poor immigrants; and rich immigrants. I also added the gender category because this issue was largely evident in who the immigrants were. Females were overwhelmingly represented as protagonists in most of the novels.

Africans. The Africans were mainly seen in a negative light. They were either "niggers," as seen in *The Slave Dancer*; jolly repulsive Negroes as seen in *My Antonia*; or cheap domestic maids who can clean houses better than women of other races, as portrayed in *Silver Days*. At first they are seen as "black gold," whose only worth is to be sold to the highest bidder. They are as cattle being used for their strength in enabling plantation owners to plant and harvest large crops. Later the portrayal is one of jolly blacks who are always as happy as children, who could be repulsive except when they had a huge grin on their faces.

While the Africans (who were later classified as Negroes, Blacks, Afro-Americans, and African Americans, to name a few) have suffered grave injustices, their contributions to making America the country it is today transcends all factions of American life. As slaves, their free labor was invaluable as croppers planted their fields and hoped for rich harvest. Slavery proved very profitable for some slave masters (Zinn 1995). Thus, the Africans' arrival in America was not beneficial to them but rather to their masters or owners. During the various American wars, many slaves fought with patriotic pride even when they knew their efforts were not acknowledged. Takaki (1993) found that the early twentieth century was still very repressive for blacks. Today, life for many African Americans still mirrors the inferior position in which they have always been placed, but many have determinedly moved above this conforming mold.

Asians. The Asians were frequently identified by "slant eyes," their "funny" dress, the foods they ate, and their overall customs, which were totally different from white Americans. They were always wary even of "good" people who offered to help them. They were frequently unforgiving, even when others made attempts to be friendly, and were ungrateful for the help of strangers.

In *The Star Fisher*, when Miss Lucy discovered that Mrs. Lee could not cook and offered to teach her, Mrs. Lee angrily refused her offer of help. Mrs. Lee was sure that Miss Lucy had "something up her sleeves" for wanting to help a complete stranger. She saw Miss Lucy's gesture of friendship as an intrusion on her family's privacy; thus, she is portrayed as an ungrateful person. There are no explanations for why Mrs. Lee felt the way she did toward her white landlady.

The history of how Chinese immigrants have been treated in America since the eighteenth century is not explained here. In *Kim/Kimi*, Kim's Japanese-American grandmother's refusal to see her even after she learns that Kim was her dead son's daughter, further emphasizes the unforgiving disposition of the immigrants.

Chinese immigrants have contributed tremendously to the improved welfare of the United States. They were overwhelmingly represented in the building of the Central Pacific Railroad, doing most of the physical labor required: laying tracks, operating power drills, and handling explosives (Takaki 1993; Wu 1982). They were also largely responsible for building the agricultural industry in California. According to Takaki, the white immigrants found the Chinese immigrants to be hardworking and frugal; thus planters felt that they were good examples for their slaves to follow. Although their contributions may not be readily acknowledged, America's many resources have been strengthened because of these immigrants' ingenuity.

Native Americans. The Native Americans are portrayed as people who have no say in how their lives are lived out in the America that white settlers built. Their every move was decided for them by others who felt that they were better than the Native Americans. In the true sense of the meaning of immigration, the Native Americans are not in the same category as the other immigrants discussed in this study. After all, they were already living in the Americas before the white settlers came and staked their claims on land that was already occupied. They are not immigrants but rather natives. This fact seems to elude many concerned with writing the history of America. Because their way of living was considerably different from the white settlers, they were ultimately the ones to be "civilized." The Native Americans are given pity but their position in early America is rarely, if ever, explained.

Native Americans' contributions to America are invaluable, although they are rarely acknowledged. When the colonists first arrived in America, they had little knowledge of how to survive in the wilderness they found. Takaki (1993) describes the terrible living conditions many of these early settlers faced. Many learned survival techniques from tribes that they forged friendships with. These tribes shared their farming and hunting techniques with the colonists, showing them the types of grains they ate. Although the ultimate relationship between the colonists and the Native Americans resulted in many tribes being wiped out completely, the help given to those early settlers enabled them to survive and others to later join them here. Corn, now a common staple in American society, is one invaluable legacy given by this embattled race.

South Americans (Latin Americans/Hispanics). The representations of the Mexicans and Salvadorans also contributed to the negative images that are commonly represented. Manny's experiences of growing up poor, orphaned, and homeless in Mexico show why he dreams daily of coming to America. However, that journey to America is portrayed as a high-risk venture that is totally unwelcomed by the Americans. The unlucky immigrants are captured and returned to Mexico only to make the attempt to cross again and again. The Salvadoran immigrants are refugees but they are not accorded the same treatment as the Cambodian and Vietnamese immigrants. They are like the Mexican immigrants, illegally vying for work and food and dependent on the kindness of strangers.

The Mexicans have contributed a lot to America. In fact, some of the vast American lands today (California and Texas) were actually gained from wars waged against Mexico. Because of this exchange of land, many native-born people became foreigners in their own land (Takaki 1993). Hispanic immigrants dominate the migrant crop workers who labor for minimal wages in the agricultural industries. Theirs is a thankless job but one that is quickly targeted whenever the nativist speeches on overrepresentation of immigrants begin. They have contributed greatly to architecture, business, and all sectors of American culture.

Whites: Western and Eastern Europeans. Many white Western and Eastern Europeans who came initially experienced race and class prejudices because the Northern Europeans, already in America, felt that immigrants who were not Northern, English-speaking people (Anglo-Saxon Protestants) were inferior. However, over time and with hard work these Western and Eastern immigrants are shown to be fully participating in the American dream, learning the Northern Europeans' way of life.

In *Journey to America* and *Silver Days*, the Platt family was from a wealthy home in Germany. They had to leave because of Nazi threats against them, and they settled in America. Initially, the family experiences hardships. The father has difficulty finding a steady job and the mother is refused domestic jobs because she is not black. Soon, however, Mr. Platt is able to start his own business and the family moves up on the socioeconomic scale.

Rebekah's family, in *Land of Hope*, leaves behind a poor lifestyle and immigrates with hopes of having a better life in America. They are pulled into the drudgery of the sweatshop life as soon as they arrive, and soon the parents seem to give up all hopes of a better life. Rebekah's determination, however, shows promise that the future will be different for the family.

Many white immigrants became slave owners as they saw an opportunity they would not have had in their own countries to own property and cultivate crops. While others were initially kept out of this socioeconomic level, over time they found themselves being accepted into the dominant groups. Many worked as indentured servants, doing many of the menial jobs that black slaves had to do. However, as soon as they had paid off their debt, they were free to move on to better things. Many could quickly overcome this humble beginning and start their lives afresh. Blumenthal (1981) asserts that America's way of life has been nourished from many sources and the contribution of Eastern Europeans is quite notable among these sources.

Gender. Although the gender issue was not a main focus of this study in that it did not stand out as forcefully as race and class in American legislation acts from 1820 to the present, it played a major role in the representation of the immigrants discussed. Of the seventeen novels analyzed, only three of the protagonists were males. Thus, the females played a major role in the types of immigrants discussed. During the early immigration years many young and unmarried girls came with their families, but a significant minority came alone, sometimes before their other family members (Friedman-Kasaba 1996). Many of these young girls put aside some of their earnings to support aging parents left behind in Europe (for example, Peggy in *Wildflower Girl*) or to assist other family members to migrate (for example, Fagel in *Good-bye to the Trees*).

While many of the girls discussed in this study also had to work hard to help their families financially, their status was often regarded below that of their brothers. This pattern seems in keeping with the historical representation of women in society. In a society defined by men, women have always been invisible and voiceless (Thompson 1994). This exclusion cuts across all sectors of life. The historical representation of the woman's position in the home is played out in the representations in the novels. Women in the lower socioeconomic classes always had to work to supplement the family's income while the women in the higher socioeconomic levels worked mainly because they wanted to do so. Antonia was hired out to work on other farms to help the family, but her pay was negotiated by, and delivered to, her brother, who determined how it was spent. Rebekah was smarter than her brothers and even though she wanted to go to college, her parents felt that an education for her would be a waste. Her future was to get married and have children. Essentially, she was to become a housewife. Sundara was capable of working to supplement the family's income, but she was not allowed to date. Her future husband would be chosen by her family. She would have no say in who this person would be.

Women constitute half the population of the country but their invisibility is a sign of their "submerged status" (Zinn 1995: 102). Friedman-Kasaba (1996) posits that there are hierarchical relations of gender, nationality, ethnicity, race, and class that are tightly interwoven within interactions between immigrant women and state migration policies. In early immigration eras, women were totally subservient to their husbands, but this sentiment has changed dramatically. Women have fought hard for their rights, taking part in various movements and conventions

(Zinn 1995). Their contribution to America's development is also often not immediately acknowledged. They worked hard during the wars, taking care of their husbands' crops, working in the factories, and filling in everywhere men could not. When many men died or returned home maimed, the women simply carried on their jobs. In essence, they were the backbone of the country's development.

Poor. Poor immigrants came to America with one fervent hope, to make something of themselves that would prove far better than the life they led back home. When Chanah's family left Poland, her father sealed five dollars' worth of gold in his shoes so it would not be stolen. This and two silver cups were the family's only financial assets. However, the father was convinced that as soon as he reached America, the family would be "richer than rich." Poor immigrants also faced more obstacles than immigrants who came with money. They were more likely to be interrogated when they arrived in New York. Rebekah's grandfather was refused entry because he had a childhood limp. Although it was not a cause for concern, the immigration officials felt he was likely to become a ward of the government. Maria and her family arrived in the United States illegally after being smuggled across the Mexican border. They joined millions of other undocumented immigrants already "draining" the states' welfare system. Poor immigrants, then, are certainly not an asset to the United States (never mind that they provide cheap and often unpaid labor in various business sectors).

Class differences have always helped to solidify the rift between "those who have" and "those who don't." While much is heard about the poor immigrants who traveled to America, in often inhumane conditions, very little is said about the rich. Poor immigrants have been a staple of America's development because they are often the ones involved in the actual "doing." They lease farms from rich sharecroppers and farm crops that ultimately are not theirs. They do the menial jobs that others find beneath them. Their jobs are also thankless because while everyone complains about their continued presence, the silent consent is that they are really needed to maintain the infrastructure of America's daily existence.

Rich. Although there were immigrants who were considered rich, in that they were able to travel in first, second, or third class and not in steerage as they crossed the Atlantic, these immigrants are generally mentioned only as a passing thought. Many of the Europeans portrayed in the novels came across in steerage, the cheapest method of travel. They were exposed to the rich immigrants only in the sense that they knew these people were traveling on the same ship. They were never allowed to intermingle, since the rich immigrants did not want to be associated in any way with the poor immigrants. When Chanah and her cousin sneaked onto the upper deck in their search for her stray cat, the sailors quickly took them back to steerage with the admonition that they were "steerage children" and did not belong in the upper deck. The Platts traveled in first class so they enjoyed catered foods, movies, and various entertainment on board. Passengers in steerage had to contend with whatever ration they were given below. There is the sense that rich immigrants are not "immigrants"; rather, their financial situation immediately affords them an "American" status. From his argument, Stein clearly does not want to see poor immigrants entering the United States. However, would people in this category (the rich who have something to offer) be welcomed with open arms? After all, these people would have money to contribute to the American economy and they would definitely not be needed to fill the "labor shortage" gap.

These various representations emphasize that the treatment and experiences of the immigrants, although generally similar, were different in some ways as well. This latter categorization looked at the immigrants' portrayal across the immigration periods. As the discussion indicates, the Hispanic immigrants seem to confirm California's hysteria that illegal immigrants are draining the state's welfare system. The Asian Americans suffer minimal racial discrimination, but as the historical data suggests, they quickly become forces to be reckoned with. The adults own businesses and the children are smart in school. The whites also suffer initial prejudice but with hard work and perseverance they are able to overcome this obstacle and soon assimilate into the dominant culture. The different ways in which the immigrants are portrayed show that along with the laws that dictated the types of immigrants America would accept, race and class issues indeed have played important roles in America's immigration policies. The premises of these books indicate that race, class, and gender issues have been, and still are, major forces in American history. The ways in which people of different racial groups acclimate to American life indicate how they are viewed in the current debates.

Overall, the representations of the immigrants in these novels could give "wings" to Stein's assertions on the value of immigrants. While the books show examples of how different immigrant groups came to America and their experiences when they got here, none really addresses the history of immigration in any detail nor explicates the reasons why the immigrants reacted the way they did to conditions they faced. The immigrants are portrayed as people coming to America "to get something from," not "to give anything to," the good of the country. Since America does not have an "acute labor shortage" and there is no longer "an empty continent" to fill, these people are no longer needed. Americans should now be able to live in peace without constantly having to worry about people coming to "take" hard-earned resources from its citizens.

Immigrant Literature: Implications of Representation

The analysis of the seventeen novels reflecting the experiences of immigrants in America indicates, as I have argued throughout this study, that race and class issues have influenced the trends in immigration policies and immigration discomfort throughout America's history. Kincheloe's (1997) assumption that nothing is neutral and that there are no truly objective ways of seeing was evident in this discussion. So, too, the premise of critical literacy, which challenges us not to accept anything as a given but rather to question ideas we are presented with, has helped to shape the lessons learned from this study.

The present debate that immigrants will eat up America's resources, or that immigrants are no longer needed in America, resounds in the history of immigration since the 1820s. When the Eastern and Southern European immigrants began arriving in America, Northern Europeans quickly differentiated themselves from these immigrants. The Northern European immigrants argued that too many new immigrants were arriving and sought ways to limit their number. Establishing a literacy test for all individuals sixteen years old and above was one means of stemming this increase. If arriving immigrants were not Anglo-Saxon Protestant English-speaking Europeans, they were the "outsiders" or the "others." Newcomers who resembled these earlier immigrants in that they had the same skin color—for example, the Irish immigrants—were initially excluded from partaking in the mainstream American culture. The outsider stigma changed to affect the newest immigrant group or groups as different immigrant groups arrived. While the white immigrants were quickly assimilated, after they were allowed to by the dominant culture, others considered as "minority" populations did not. Over the years, many of these minority groups have been allowed to participate in various factions of the American mainstream culture, but their differences are still upheld. Today, immigrants are still coming in great numbers but their racial makeup has changed. This causes great concern for people like Dan Stein. Americans have argued for "English only" communications, and various educational programs have been implemented to separate these latest groups of immigrants. People are uncomfortable about the changing racial makeup of many major cities. Immigration proves to be a code for race and class in the United States' immigration agenda.

The analysis of the immigrant novels reveals that while these books are intended to educate others about the experiences of immigrants in America, these texts cannot be left alone to speak for themselves. The books are great reading materials that may illuminate historical events of which many people are unaware as they read dominant history—for example, the experiences of Japanese Americans in the 1940s—but they also have limits. If these books are intended for use by young children who will be reading about race and class issues at a sophisticated level, then the limits of these novels must be challenged.

A majority of the novels are negative reflections of how American society treats its "other." They serve to reproduce existing social formations that if immigrants are not from the mainstream culture—white people—they are exotic creatures whose experiences differ extensively from those of the first immigrants who arrived on American shores. Books being used to present the "other" to American children need to move beyond this reflection to promote a democratic and emancipatory change. They should not seek to reinforce stereotypes (Banks 1997; Lamme 1996) but rather should provide examples of contrasting views.

Experiences with immigrant literature should provide valid generalizations and theories about the characteristics of ethnic groups (Banks 1997). Banks further asserts that children should learn about both past and present experiences of immigrants and explore why there are differences in experiences. Curriculum cannot be transformed by simply adding books reflecting immigrants' experiences. A more conscious effort to integrate these materials is needed. While it is good to show the negative experiences of immigrants, this representation should be followed by or represented in conjunction with positive experiences.

America is a nation of immigrants (Ashabranner 1993). This means that while many immigrant groups have existed in the United States for many generations and they are no longer regarded as immigrants, historical data indicates that at some point in the past, they had immigrants in the family. While the current debate about immigrants in America is centered on members of minority populations and on how these people do not "fit" the dominant American profile, the current trends in immigration indicate that the dominant population is changing (Banks 1997; Nieto 1996). People of "minority" classifications are now the majority in terms of population in several large cities across the United States. America will continue to be a nation of immigrants.

A critical sociology of literature framework is a viable tool that can carve out for us how representations of immigrants affect the presentation of different people to others. While I have ascertained that race and class issues were and still are important factors in how immigrants are represented in history and in literature, I believe that their continued presence indicates that there is much work to be done if all persons involved are to participate in a democratic, equal opportunity society. Since authors make ideological decisions in the types of images they project in the books they write and since teachers and others involved in the education of young minds make decisions about the types of materials these children will read, the decision for the types of materials to be used rests with all involved. Although it is impossible to eradicate centuries of racial and class discrimination in one generation, the process must begin somewhere. The continued presence of racial and class discrimination proves true the old adage: "Those who cannot remember the past are condemned to repeat it." In order for us to interrupt this cyclical treatment of immigrants, we need to be aware of the history of immigration in America, of the role politics plays in determining that history, and determinedly work as one to ensure that negative experiences and connotations of immigrants do not continue to be replicated generation after generation. Otherwise, sentiments like those expressed by Dan Stein will continue to reinforce the "worthlessness" of immigrants in the United States.

References

Albrecht, Milton C. 1954. "The Relationship of Literature and Society." *American Journal of Sociology* 49: 425–436.

"All Right Just This Once." 1994. *Economist*, 30 April: 31.

American Legion Magazine. 1995. "Do We Need More Immigrants? No Bar the Door." April 138, (4), 26–28.

Anderson, Gary L., and Patricia Irvine. 1993. "Informing Critical Literacy With Ethnography." In *Critical Literacy: Politics, Praxis, and the Postmodern*, edited by Colin Lankshear and Peter L. McLaren. Albany: State University of New York.

Apple, Michael W. 1993. "Constructing the 'Other': Rightist Reconstructions of Common Sense." In *Race Identity an Representation in Education*, edited by Cameron McCarthy and Warren Crichlow. New York: Routledge.

Aronowitz, Stanley. 1992. *The Politics of Identity, Class, Culture, Social Movements*. New York: Routledge.

Ashabranner, Brent. 1993. *Still a Nation of Immigrants*. New York: Cobblehill/ Dutton.

Bandon, Alexandra. 1993. *Mexican Americans*. New York: New Discovery.

———. 1994. *West Indian Americans*. New York: New Discovery.

Banks, James, A. 1987. *Teaching Strategies for Ethnic Studies*. 4th ed. Boston: Allyn and Bacon.

———. 1993. "Multicultural Education: Progress and Prospects." *Phi Delta Kappan,* 75 (1): 21.

————. 1994a. *An Introduction to Multicultural Education.* Needham, MA: Allyn and Bacon.

————. 1994b. *Multiethnic Education: Theory and Practice.* 3d ed. Needham, MA: Allyn and Bacon.

————. 1995. *Handbook of Research on Multicultural Education.* New York: Simon and Schuster.

————. 1997. *Teaching Strategies for Ethnic Studies.* 6th ed. Needham, MA: Allyn and Bacon.

Barkan, Elliott R. 1996. *And Still They Come: Immigrants and American Society 1920 to the 1990s.* Wheeling, IL: Harlan Davidson.

Beilenson, Anthony. 1996. "Time to Address Effects of Immigration on U.S. Population." *Chicago Tribune*, 13 November: 21.

Bennett, Christine I. 1995. *Comprehensive Multicultural Education: Theory and Practice.* 3d ed. Needham, MA: Allyn and Bacon.

Blumenthal, Shirley. 1981. *Coming to America: Immigrants from Eastern Europe.* New York: Delacorte Press.

Braham, Carol G., ed. 1996. *Random House: Webster's Dictionary.* New York: Ballantine.

Brownstone, David. 1988a. *The Chinese-American Heritage.* New York: Facts on File.

————. 1988b. *The Jewish-American Heritage.* New York: Facts on File.

————. 1989. *The Irish-American Heritage.* New York: Facts on File.

Chandler, David. 1991. *The Land and People of Cambodia.* New York: HarperCollins.

Christensen, Linda. 1996. "How My Students Taught Me About Immigration: What Happened to the Golden Door?" *Rethinking Schools* 11 (Fall 1): 1, 4–5, 20–21.

Courts, Patrick L. 1997. *Multicultural Literacies: Dialects, Discourse, and Diversity*. New York: Peter Lang.

De Garza, Patricia. 1973. *Chicanos: The Story of Mexican Americans*. New York: Julian Messner.

DeGeorge, Gail. 1994. "How Many People Can We Absorb?" *Business Week:* 26 September: 48A–48E.

Delpit, Lisa. 1992. "Acquisition of Literate Discourse: Bowing Before the Master?" *Theory into Practice XXXI* (Autumn 4): 298–302.

Dill, Bonnie T. 1994. "Race, Class, and Gender: Prospects for an All-Inclusive Sisterhood." In *The Education Feminism Reader*, edited by Lynda Stone. New York: Routledge.

D'Souza, Dinesh. 1995. *The End of Racism: Principles from a Multiracial Society.* New York: Free Press.

Easterlin, Richard A., David Ward, William S. Bernard, and Reed Ueda. 1982. *Immigration: Dimensions of Ethnicity*. Cambridge: Harvard University Press.

Enciso, Patricia E. 1994. "Cultural Identity and Response to Literature: Running Lessons From Maniac Magee." *Language Arts* 71: 524–535.

First, Joan M. 1988. "Immigrant Students in U.S. Public Schools: Challenges with Solutions." *Phi Delta Kappan* 70: 205–210.

Freedman, Russell. 1980. *Immigrant Kids*. New York: Scholastic Inc.

Friedman-Kasaba, Kathie. 1996. *Memories of Migration: Gender, Ethnicity and Work in the Lives of Jewish and Italian Women in New*

York, 1870–1924. New York: State University of New York Press, Albany.

Giroux, Henry A. 1994. "Living Dangerously: Identity Politics and the New Cultural Racism." In *Between Borders: Pedagogy and the Politics of Cultural Studies,* edited by Henry A. Giroux and Peter McLaren. New York: Routledge.

Giroux, Henry, and Peter McLaren, eds. 1994. *Between Borders: Pedagogy and the Politics of Cultural Studies.* New York: Routledge.

Glazer, Nathan. 1995. "Immigration and the American Future." *Public Interest* 118 (Winter): 45–60.

Gould, Stephen J. 1981. *The Mismeasure of Man.* New York: W. W. Norton & Co.

Gresson, Aaron D., III. 1995. *The Recovery of Race in America.* Minneapolis: University of Minnesota Press.

———. 1996. "Postmodern America and the Multicultural Crisis: Reading Forrest Gump as the 'Call Back to Whiteness.'" *Taboo*:11–34.

———. 1997. "Identity, Class, and Teacher Education: The Persistence of 'Class Effects' in the Classroom." *The Review of Education/Pedagogy/Cultural Studies* 19: 335–348.

Grossman, Ronald. 1966. *The Italians in America.* Minneapolis: Lerner.

Grunfeld, Uriel J. 1997. "Representing the Holocaust on Film: *Schindler's List* and the Pedagogy of Popular Memory.*"* Ph.D. diss., Pennsylvania State University.

Hade, Daniel D. 1997. "Reading Multiculturally." In *Using Multiethnic Literature in the K–8 Classroom,* edited by Violet J. Harris. New York: Christopher-Gordon.

Hall, John. 1979. *The Sociology of Literature.* New York: Longman.

Harris, Violet. 1991. "Multicultural Curriculum: African American Children's Literature." *Young Children* 46: 37–44.

Heer, David. 1996. *Immigration in America's Future: Social Science Findings and the Policy Debate*. Boulder, CO: Westview.

Hoerder, Dirk, and Diethelm Knauf, eds. 1992. *Fame, Fortune and Sweet Liberty: The Great European Emigration*. New York: Temmen.

Hopkins, Mary C.1996. *Braving a New World: Cambodian (Khmer) Refugees in an American City*. Westport, CT: Bergin & Garvey.

Huck, Charlotte; Susan Hepler, and Janet Hickman. 1993. *Children's Literature in the Elementary School*. Orlando: Harcourt Brace & Co.

Ignatiev, Noel.1995.*How the Irish Became White*. New York: Routledge.

Jackson, Jesse, and Elaine Landau. 1973. *Black in America: A Fight for Freedom*. New York: Julian Messner.

"Judge Rules Against Proposition 187." 1997. *United Press International* (14 November).

Keely, Charles B. 1986. "Issues in Immigration Since 1965." *Social Education*, 50: 178–182.

Kellogg, John. 1988. "Forces of Change." *Phi Delta Kappan:* 199–204.

Kelly, Gail P. 1977. *From Vietnam to America: A Chronicle of the Vietnamese Immigration to the United States*. Boulder, CO: Westview.

Kincheloe, Joe L. 1993. *Toward a Critical Politics of Teacher Thinking: Mapping the Postmodern*. Westport, CT: Bergin & Garvey.

———. 1997. "Fiction Formulas: Critical Constructionism and the Representation of Reality." In *Representation and the Text: Re-framing the Narrative Voice*, edited by W. G. Tierney and Yvonna S. Lincoln. Albany: State University of New York Press.

Kincheloe, Joe L., and Peter L. McLaren. 1994. "Rethinking Critical Theory and Qualitative Research." In *Handbook of Qualitative Research* edited by Norman Denzin and Yvonna Lincoln. Thousand Oaks, CA: Sage.

Kincheloe, Joe L., and Shirley R. Steinberg. 1997. *Changing Multiculturalism*. Philadelphia: Open University Press.

Kunz, Virginia B. 1966. *The French in America*. Minneapolis: Lerner.

Kuropas, Myron. 1972. *The Ukrainians in America*. Minneapolis: Lerner.

Lamm, Richard D. 1995. "Enough." *Across the Board* 32 (March):35–37.

Lamme, Linda L. 1996. "Digging Deeply: Morals and Ethics in Children's Literature." *Journal for a Just & Caring Education* 2: 411–419.

Lankshear, Colin, and Peter L. McLaren, eds. 1993. *Critical Literacy: Politics, Praxis, and the Postmodern*. Albany: State University of New York.

Laurenson, Diana T., and Alan Swingewood. 1972. *The Sociology of Literature*. New York: Schocken Books.

Lopata, Helana Z. 1994. *Polish Americans*. New Brunswick, NJ: Transaction Publishers.

Lorde, Audre. 1984. *Sister Outsider: Essays & Speeches*. Trumansburg, NY: Crossing Press.

Macedo, Donaldo. 1994. *Literacies of Power*. Boulder: Westview.

Mahler, Sarah. 1995. *Salvadorans in Suburbia: Symbiosis and Conflict*. Needham Heights, MA: Allyn and Bacon.

May, Jill P. 1995. *Children's Literature and Critical Theory*. New York: Oxford University Press.

McKellar, Barbara. 1994. "Only the Fittest of the Fittest Will Survive: Black Women and Education." In *The Education Feminism Reader,* edited by Lynda Stone. New York: Routledge.

McLaren, Peter, and Colin Lankshear. 1993. "Critical Literacy and the Postmodern Turn." In *Critical Literacy: Politics, Praxis, and the Postmodern*, edited by Colin Lankshear and Peter L. McLaren. Albany: State University of New York.

Miller, Harris N. 1995. "Don't Close the Door on Immigrant Programmers." *Computerworld,* 10 July: 37.

Morawska, Ewa. 1990. "The Sociology and Historiography of Immigration." In *Immigration Reconsidered: History, Sociology, and Politics,* edited by Virginia Yans-McLaughlin. New York: Oxford University Press.

Morrison, Toni. 1992. *Playing in the Dark: Whiteness and the Literary Imagination.* New York: Vintage.

Mosse, George L. 1996. *The Image of Man: The Creation of Modern Masculinity.* New York: Oxford University Press.

Nelkin, Dorothy. 1995. "Making America Safe From 'Foreign Germs.'" *Health Affairs*, 14 (Spring): 316–317.

Nelson, Murry R., and Jamie Myers. 1993. "Teaching Ethnic Cultures: Fiction and Fact." *Teaching Education* 5: 21–31.

Ng, Roxana. 1993. "Racism, Sexism, and Nation Building in Canada." In *Race Identity and Representation in Education,* edited by Cameron McCarthy and Warren Crichlow. New York: Routledge.

Nieto, Sonia. 1996. *Affirming Diversity: The Sociopolitical Context of Multicultural Education.* New York: Longman.

Nodelman, Perry. 1992. *The Pleasures of Children's Literature.* White Plains, NY: Longman.

Norton, Donna E. 1983. *Through the Eyes of a Child: An Introduction to Children's Literature*. Columbus, OH: Charles E. Merrill.

Nowakowski, Jacek. 1989. *Polish-American Ways: Recipes & Traditions*. New York: Harper & Row.

O'Brien, David J., and Stephen S. Fugita. 1991. *The Japanese American Experience*. Bloomington: Indiana University Press.

Oliver, Donald W., and Fred M. Newmann. 1967. *The Immigrant's Experience: Cultural Variety and the "Melting Pot."* Middletown, CT: Xerox Education Publications.

Patrick, John J. 1986. "Immigration in the Curriculum." *Social Education* 50: 172–176.

Peim, Nick. 1993. *Critical Theory and the English Teacher*. New York: Routledge.

Reimer, Kathryn M. 1992. "Multiethnic Literature: Holding Fast to Dreams." *Language Arts* 69: 14–21.

Rochman, Hazel. 1993. *Against Borders: Promoting Books for a Multicultural World*. Chicago: American Library Association.

Roediger, David R. 1991. *The Wages of Whiteness: Race and the Making of the American Working Class*. New York: Verso.

Rolph, Elizabeth S. 1992. *Immigration Politics: Legacy from the 1980s and Issues for the 1990s*. Santa Monica, CA: Rand.

Rothstein, Stanley W. 1994. *Schooling the Poor: A Social Inquiry into the American Educational Experience*. Westport, CT: Bergin & Garvey.

Scheurich, James. 1993. "Toward a White Discourse on White Racism." *Educational Researcher* 22: 5–10.

Schiller, Laura. 1996. "Coming to America: Community From Diversity." *Language Arts* 73: 46–51.

Shannon, George. 1988. "Making a Home of One's Own: The Young in Cross-cultural Fiction." *English Journal* 77: 14–19.

Shannon, Patrick. 1992. "Overt and Covert Censorship of Children's Books." In *Becoming Political: Readings and Writings in the Politics of Literacy Education*, edited by Patrick Shannon. Portsmouth, NH: Heinemann.

———. 1994. "I Am the Canon: Finding Ourselves in Multiculturalism." *Journal of Children's Literature* 20 (Spring): 1–5.

———. 1995. *Text, Lies and Videotape*. Portsmouth, NH: Heinemann.

Sharry, Frank. 1994. "Myths, Realities and Solutions." *Spectrum: The Journal of State Government* 67 (Winter 1): 20–26.

Short, Kathy G. 1995. *Research & Professional Resources in Children's Literature: Piecing a Patchwork Quilt*. Newark, DE: International Reading Association.

Short, Kathy G., and Kathryn M. Pierce, eds. 1990. *Talking About Books: Creating Literate Communities*. Portsmouth, NH: Heinemann.

Simon, Roger I. 1992. "Empowerment as a Pedagogy of Possibility." In *Becoming Political: Readings and Writings in the Politics of Literacy Education*, edited by Patrick Shannon. Portsmouth, NH: Heinemann.

Sims, Rudine. 1982. *Shadow and Substance*. Urbana, IL: National Council of Teachers of English.

———. 1983. "Strong Black Girls: A Ten-Year-Old Responds to Fiction About Afro-Americans." *Journal of Research and Development in Education* 16: 21–28.

Takaki, Ronald. 1993. *A Different Mirror: A History of Multicultural America*. Boston: Little, Brown and Co.

Thompson, Patricia J. 1994. Beyond Gender: Equity Issues for Home Economics Education. In *The Education Feminism Reader,* edited by Lynda Stone. New York: Routledge.

Topolnicki, Denise M. 1995. "The Real Immigrant Story: Making It Big in America." *Money* 24 (January): 128–138.

Valli, Linda. 1995. "The Dilemma of Race: Learning to be Color Blind and Color Conscious." *Journal of Teacher Education* 46: 120–129.

West, Cornel. 1993. *Race Matters*. New York: Vintage.

Wu, William F. 1982. *The Yellow Peril: Chinese Americans in American Fiction 1850–1940*. Hamden, CT: Archon.

Wytrwal, Joseph A. 1969. *The Poles in America*. Minneapolis: Lerner.

Yans-McLaughlin, Virginia, ed. 1990. *Immigration Reconsidered: History, Sociology, and Politics*. New York: Oxford University Press.

Young, Lola. 1996. *Fear of the Dark: Race, Gender and Sexuality in the Cinema*. New York: Routledge.

Ziegler, Benjamin M. 1953. *Immigration an American Dilemma: Problems in American Civilization*. Boston: D. C. Heath & Co.

Zinn, Howard. 1995. *A People's History of the United States 1492–Present*. New York: HarperCollins.

Children's Books Cited

Buss, Fran L. 1991. *Journey of the Sparrows*. New York: Bantam Doubleday Dell.

Cather, Willa. 1918. *My Antonia*. New York: Houghton Mifflin.

Conlon-McKenna, Marita. 1991. *Wildflower Girl*. New York: Puffin.

Crew, Linda. 1989. *Children of the River*. New York: Dell.

Fox, Paula. 1973. *The Slave Dancer*. New York: Bantam Doubleday Dell.

Guy, Rosa. 1973. *The Friends*. New York: Bantam Doubleday Dell.

Hesse, Karen. 1992. *Letters from Rifka*. New York: Trumpet Club.

Irwin, Hadley. 1987. *Kim/Kimi*. New York: Puffin.

Levitin, Sonia. 1970. *Journey to America*. New York: Aladdin.

———. 1989. *Silver Days*. New York: Aladdin.

Lingard, Joan. 1991. *Between Two Worlds*. New York: Puffin.

Mayerson, Evelyn W. 1990. *The Cat Who Escaped from Steerage*. New York: Macmillan.

Mohr, Nicholasa. 1989. *Going Home*. New York: Bantam Skylark.

Nixon, Joan L. 1992. *Land of Hope*. New York: Bantam Doubleday Dell.

O'Dell, Scott. 1970. *Sing Down the Moon*. New York: Dell.

Paulsen, Gary. 1987. *The Crossing*. New York: Bantam Doubleday Dell.

Shiefman, Vicky. 1993. *Good-bye to the Trees*. New York: Macmillan.

Skurzynski, Gloria. 1992. *Good-bye Billy Radish.* New York: Aladdin.

Wartski, Maureen C. 1980. *A Boat to Nowhere*. New York: Signet.

Yep, Laurence. 1991. *The Star Fisher*. New York: Puffin.

Index